Circulation policies of academic libraries in the United States, 1968

A report by the
Circulation Control Committee
LAD Section on Circulation Services

LIBRARY ADMINISTRATION DIVISION
American Library Association
Chicago, 1970

LC 71-118197

Standard Book Number 8389-5250-X (1970)

Printed in the United States of America

Contents

	Pages
Introduction........................	I - III
Questionnaire	IV - VII

Summaries

Section	I - Open or Closed Stacks......	I
Section	II - Total Circulation..........	2
Section	III - Borrowers.................	3 - 7
Section	IV - Per Capita Circulation.....	8
Section	V - Loan Periods..............	9 - 23
Section	VI - Renewals..................	24 - 25
Section	VII - Overdue Correspondence.....	26 - 54
Section	VIII - Overdue Charges...........	55 - 86
Section	IX - The Relationship Between Fines and the Return of Books......................	87 - 91

Introduction

In 1968 the Circulation Services Section of the Library Administration Division, ALA, found that little information on fines and related subjects appeared in professional literature. Several libraries had gathered some information in local or regional areas, but no information was available on practices throughout the United States.

The Section decided to do a survey to summarize practices of charges, frequency of notices, collection practices, and related information. The survey was designed to find the most common fine rates, the purpose of fines, the effects of charging or removing fines, common frequencies of sending overdue notices, and the effects of their timing, and methods of collecting books when notices fail.

Questionnaires were forwarded by the Library Technology Program office to a sampling of academic libraries and public libraries throughout the United States, its possessions, and protectorates. This report is a summarization of the information received from academic libraries. A separate report will be published for data received from public libraries.

The survey questionnaire was sent to 707 academic libraries. Replies were received from 444 institutions, but 14 of the replies were too incomplete to be used and one reply was received inadvertently from a two year college. Only degree granting institutions were included in the report.

The 429 academic libraries represented 28 percent of the total number of degree granting institutions listed in the 10th edition (1968) of American Colleges and Universities.

In most respects the questionnaire, reproduced on the pages following, is concise, pertinent and meaningful, at least in the opinion of the committee. In a few areas, however, the questions could have been more detailed and/or specific.

The question pertaining to circulation should have referred specifically to the main library, or should have stated exactly what information was desired. The committee member who worked with the academic questionnaires had no choice but to take the figures as they were given.

Question 3b, of course, was redundant.

Question 4 should have included a part for "other borrowers," because almost all universities and many colleges have patrons who are not faculty or students of the parent institution.

Question 8b might better have been worded: "Do you think that fines are an effective means of encouraging the prompt return of books?"

When working with a fairly large number of replies, and particularly when they are of a widely ranging nature, it is desirable to arrange them in some order, and to follow this order throughout the compilation and evaluation. In this case the questionnaires were arranged in descending order of annual circulation, because it seemed desirable to compare very large, large, medium and small academic libraries. Here, of course, it is assumed that circulation accurately reflects the size of both the library and its parent institution. And for the most part it did. Thus, the libraries were arranged as follows:

Class 1 - annual circulation of
200,000 or more volumes...................34 replies

Class 2 - annual circulation of
75,000 to 199,999 volumes.................75 replies

Class 3 - annual circulation of
25,000 to 74,999 volumes.................133 replies

Class 4 - annual circulation of
0 (non-circulating library)
to 24,999 volumes.......................150 replies

Class 5 - circulation figures not
given in reply.......................... 37 replies

In addition, within each of the five classes, the libraries were separated into categories - libraries of private institutions and those of public institutions. This was done so that the two basic types of institutions could be compared.

An attempt was made to divide the institutions by relative location, i.e., urban and rural. The idea here was to attempt to determine the impact, if any, upon urban institutions by outside users. Attempts to make this division, however, proved to be too subjective, and, in addition, we had not asked for the number of outside users; therefore the attempt was abandoned.

Classes and Categories		Number of Libraries Reporting		
Class		Private	Public	Total
1 (200,000 or more)		13	21	34
2 (75,000 to 199,999)		25	50	75
3 (25,000 to 74,999)		99	34	133
4 (0 to 24,999)		109	41	150
5 (not given)		26	11	37
	Total	272	157	429

The summary tables are self-explanatory. Comments of the committee are included in each section with the summary tables.

The committee wishes to express its appreciation to all librarians who participated in the survey for their interest and cooperation.

The committee also expresses its thanks to Mr. Forrest Carhart of the Library Technology Program office of ALA for their assistance in editing, producing, and distributing the questionnaires.

Inquiries and comments regarding the data should be addressed to Mr. Matt T. Roberts, Chief, Circulation Department, Washington University Library, St. Louis, Missouri, who prepared the summary.

Respectfully submitted:

CIRCULATION CONTROL COMMITTEE

Lucille Arceneaux, Lafayette Public Library
Lafayette, Louisiana

Edwin G. Jackson, Hartford Public Library
Hartford, Connecticut

Robert R. McClarren, North Suburban Regional Library System
Morton Grove, Illinois

Leo R. Rift, Ithaca College Library
Ithaca, New York

Matt T. Roberts, Washington University Library
St. Louis, Missouri

Jerry F. Young, Wisconsin Department of Public Instruction
Madison, Wisconsin

Viola B. Metternich, Public Library of Cincinnati
Cincinnati, Ohio
Chairman

Dear Librarian:

This questionnaire is being sent to you in response to a demand
expressed in requests addressed to ALA Headquarters, state library
agencies, and library publications for comprehensive information
on current library circulation practices. There is presently a
dearth of such information.

Completed questionnaires will be tabulated by the Circulation
Control Committee of the Library Administration Division's Section
on Circulation Services. Results will be analyzed and a report
written for publication in a library periodical.

Please answer all questions as fully as possible. Two copies of
the questionnaire and an addressed envelope are enclosed. One is
your file copy; the other is to be returned as soon as possible,
but no later than May 1.

Thank you for your cooperation.

Viola Metternich, Chairman
Circulation Control Committee
LAD

VM:ls

Encl.

COLLEGE AND UNIVERSITY LIBRARY QUESTIONNAIRE

Name of College or University_____

Name of Library_____

Street address_____

City_____ State_____ Zip_____

Name and title of person completing questionnaire_____

1a. Public college or university?_____

1b. Private college or university?_____

2. Circulation in 1967 (or last 12 months available)_____

3a. Open stacks? Yes____ No____   3b. Closed stacks? Yes____ No____

4. Population served (full time equivalent)

    a. Faculty_____

    b. Graduate students_____

    c. Undergraduates_____

5. LOANS	Over Night	1 Day	5 Days	7 Days	14 Days	28 Days	Other (Specify)
Books:							
Faculty							
Graduate students							
Undergraduates							
Periodicals:							
Faculty							
Graduate students							
Undergraduates							
Pamphlets:							
Faculty							
Graduate students							
Undergraduates							
Reserve books							

6. RENEWALS

	Permitted by Phone		Permitted by Presenting Book at Library	
	Yes	No	Yes	No
General stack books				
Reserve books				
Periodicals				
Pamphlets				

7. OVERDUES

a. Type of Notice

	1st Notice	2nd Notice	3rd Notice	4th Notice	Additional Notice (Specify)
Written notice					
Telephone					
Faculty advisor					
Dean's office					
Messenger					
Other (Please specify)					

b. Length of Time Between Each Notice

	1 day	3 days	5 days	7 days	14 days	21 days	28 days	Other (Specify)
Time from due date to 1st notice								
1st to 2nd notice								
2nd to 3rd notice								
3rd to 4th notice								
4th to 5th notice								
Other (Specify)								

Note: If any notice checked in the column of the number of days is different from specific choice given, write in correct number of days.

c. Total of overdue notices sent in a year? 1st_____   2nd_____   3rd_____

8a. <u>FINES</u>

What fines do you charge per day?	1¢	2¢	3¢	4¢	5¢	10¢	15¢	20¢	25¢	Other (Specify)
General stack books										
Reserve books										
Periodicals										
Pamphlets										

b. Do you think there is a relation between fines and book return? Yes____ No____

Comments:_____

_____

_____

_____

_____

_____

I. OPEN OR CLOSED STACKS

Although not stated in the questionnaire, the replies were assumed
to be in reference to the general book stack. Almost all academic
libraries have some books that are not directly accessible to users.
These would include "rare books" and some "reserve" books.

Class	Category	Open Stacks	Closed Stacks	Both[1]	no answer
1	Private	10 (77%)[2]	2 (15%)	1 (8%)	0
	Public	16 (76%)	5 (24%)	0	0
	total	26 (76%)	7 (21%)	1 (3%)	0
2	Private	23 (92%)	2 (8%)	0	0
	Public	44 (88%)	4 (8%)	2 (4%)	0
	total	67 (89%)	6 (8%)	2 (3%)	0
3	Private	94 (95%)	2 (2%)	1 (1%)	2 (2%)
	Public	33 (97%)	0	1 (3%)	0
	total	127 (95%)	2 (2%)	2 (2%)	2 (2%)
4	Private	105 (96%)	3 (3%)	1 (1%)	0
	Public	38 (93%)	2 (5%)	0	1 (2%)
	total	143 (95%)	5 (3%)	1 (1%)	1 (1%)
5	Private	25 (96%)	0	1 (4%)	0
	Public	10 (91%)	0	1 (9%)	0
	total	35 (95%)	0	2 (5%)	0
Total	Private	257 (94%)	9 (3%)	4 (2%)	2 (1%)
	Public	141 (90%)	11 (7%)	4 (3%)	1 (-)
	Total	398 (93%)	20 (5%)	8 (2%)	3 (-)

1 Open to faculty and graduate students, closed to undergraduate students.

2 All percentages, here and throughout the report, are rounded to the nearest
significant figure.

II. TOTAL CIRCULATION

The figures given below are, or are assumed to be, for general stack
books only. Many libraries listed separate figures for reserve books
and the like. Where libraries did not indicate otherwise, the figures
given were assumed to be for general stack books.

Class	Private	Public	Total
1	3,959,278	8,563,354	12,522,632
2	3,186,026	6,352,767	9,538,793
3	4,285,322	1,665,670	5,950,992
4	1,365,067	442,279	1,807,346
Total	12,795,693	17,024,070	29,819,763

Mean and median circulation by class and category. (Mean and median
figures were derived from libraries reporting circulation figures -
246 private and 146 public, or a total of 392 of the 429 replies received.)

Class	Private		Public		Total	
	mean	median	mean	median	mean	median
1	304,560	250,000	407,799	313,872	368,314	294,880
2	127,441	134,345	127,055	125,392	127,184	126,229
3	43,286	40,735	48,988	51,287	44,744	41,874
4	15,524	14,126	10,787	10,254	12,049	13,317
Total	52,015	27,169	116,603	71,782	76,071	34,453

It is interesting that in the figures for all libraries, the mean
(average) is considerably higher than the median (mid-point). This
indicates the influence of class 1 on the mean and class 4 on the
median. Overall, class 4, by its very size, lowered the median,
but class 1 had a relatively greater effect on the mean.

If our sample accurately reflects the circulation of all 1,546
academic libraries under consideration, we can state that, in
the year of the sample, the 1,546 institutions' circulation was
117,605,766 volumes from their general book stacks.

One librarian reported (perhaps with some humor) that his circulation was 8,200 + reserves + theft.

2

III. BORROWERS

A. Faculty

Class	Private		Public		Both	
	number reporting	number of faculty	number reporting	number of faculty	number reporting	number of faculty
1	13	13,312	19	26,213	32	39,525
2	24	12,640	49	29,578	73	42,218
3	96	11,198	34	7,203	130	18,401
4	106	5,568	37	4,047	143	9,615
5	23	2,931	11	4,268	34	7,199
TOTAL	262	45,649	150	71,309	412	116,958

Class	Private		Public		Both	
	mean	median	mean	median	mean	median
1	1,024	1,000	1,380	1,000	1,235	1,000
2	527	512	604	350	578	366
3	117	87	212	181	142	100
4	52	45	109	64	67	49
5	127	50	388	238	212	62
ALL	174	70	475	245	284	85

Once again, we see how a relatively few institutions at the top end of the
scale have a considerable effect on the mean, whereas the relatively large
number of institutions of smaller size influence the median. The private
institutions show a more gradual and consistent decrease in faculty numbers,
especially in classes 1 and 2, than do the public institutions. In class
2, public, the difference between mean and median is particularly striking.
It is also quite striking in class 5, private, but had these institutions
recorded circulation figures, they probably would have been spread fairly
evenly throughout the other four classes.

III. Borrowers

B. Graduate students

Class	Private		Public		Total	
	number reporting[1]	number of students	number reporting	number of students	number reporting	number of students
1	13	42,965	19	64,310	32	107,275
2	24	30,621	49	42,747	73	73,368
3	96	6,500	34	7,748	130	13,948
4	106	4,031	40	10,481	146	14,512
5	24	5,567	11	14,544	35	20,111
Total	263	89,684	153	139,530	416	229,214

Class	Private		Public		Total	
	mean	median	mean	median	mean	median
1	3,305	3,117	3,384	2,224	3,352	2,709
2	1,276	1,033	872	570	1,005	786
3	68	0	219	78	107	0
4	38	0	262	0	99	0
5	232	0	1,322	450	575	0
Total	341	0	912	252	551	0^2

1 Includes those reporting that they had no graduate students.

2 A median of 0 indicates that at least one more than half of the reporting institutions had no graduate students.

The fact that so many of the reporting institutions had no graduate
students makes it pointless to attempt any interpretation, except
for classes 1 and 2. Here again, we see that there is far more
consistency between mean and median in the private institutions.

III. Borrowers

   C. Undergraduate students

Class	Private		Public		Total	
	number reporting	number of students	number reporting	number of students	number reporting	number of students
1	13	71,036	20	274,267	33	345,303
2	24	125,862	49	313,297	73	439,159
3	97	135,511	33	96,971	130	232,482
4	105	67,150	39	75,067	144	142,217
5	24	31,418	11	51,906	35	83,324
Total	263	430,977	152	811,508	415	1,242,485

Class	Private		Public		Total	
	mean	median	mean	median	mean	median
1	5,464	4,464	13,713	12,090	10,464	9,480
2	5,244	3,693	6,394	5,340	6,016	5,000
3	1,397	1,074	2,939	2,300	1,788	1,265
4	640	600	1,925	972	988	637
5	1,309	800	4,719	2,171	2,381	1,094
Total	1,639	900	5,339	3,089	2,994	913

Although it is hardly surprising that the average undergraduate
enrollment in the public institutions is greater than in the
private, it is somewhat surprising that it is 3.2 times as great.
Oddly, except for classes 4 and 5, there seems to be more consistency between mean and median in the public than in the private
institutions.

III. Borrowers

D. All borrowers

Class	Private		Public		Total	
	number reporting	number of borrowers	number reporting	number of borrowers	number reporting	number of borrowers
1	13	127,313	19 1/3[1]	364,790	32 1/3	492,103
2	24	169,123	49	385,622	73	554,745
3	96 1/3	153,209	33 2/3	111,622	130	264,831
4	105 2/3	76,749	38 2/3	89,595	144 1/3	166,344
5	23 2/3	39,916	11	70,718	34 2/3	110,634
Total	262 2/3	566,394	151 2/3	1,022,347	414 1/3	1,588,657
classes 1-4 only[2]	239	526,394	140 2/3	951,629	379 2/3	1,478,023

Class	Private		Public		Total	
	mean	median	mean	median	mean	median
1	9,793	8,655	18,872	16,009	15,221	12,241
2	7,047	5,473	7,870	6,449	7,599	6,179
3	1,590	1,205	3,315	2,484	2,037	1,475
4	726	650	2,317	1,040	1,153	704
5	1,686	850	6,429	2,514	3,191	1,322
Total	2,156	975	6,741	4,097	3,834	1,409

1 Fractions occur when a library does not report all **three types** of borrowers. For example, if a library reported only the number of graduate students, and not the number of faculty and under-graduates; it would be counted in the total for all borrowers as 1/3.

2 Totals for classes 1-4 only will be used in computing per capita borrowing.

6

III. Borrowers

E. Ratio of faculty to all students - expressed as 1:

Class	Private	Public	Total
1	1:8.5	1:12.4	1:11.2
2	1:12.4	1:12.0	1:12.1
3	1:12.5	1:14.9	1:13.3
4	1:13.0	1:20.1	1:16.2
5	1:12.1	1:15.5	1:13.9
Total	1:11.1	1:13.2	1:12.5

The ratio of faculty to students is almost uniformly lower in the private institutions, and tends to be lower in the larger institutions.

The latter observation might make us jump to a quick (and dangerous) conclusion. If we hypothesize that the faculty of the smaller institutions do more teaching and less research than their counterparts in the larger institutions (i.e., the "public or perish" doctrine is more prevalent in the larger places), it would seem to follow that the smaller colleges and universities should have a higher ratio of faculty to students. Unfortunately, we lack the information necessary even to make the hypothesis, much less prove it.

IV. Per capita circulation (general stack books - all borrowers)

Class		Private	Public	Total
	Range	6.3 - 385.5	7.8 - 75.8	6.3 - 385.5
1	Mean	31.1	21.6	24.2
	Median	27.8	22.3	25.4
	Range	3.9 - 69.7	5.4 - 52.9	3.9 - 69.7
2	Mean	18.1	16.1	16.7
	Median	24.4	18.6	19.9
	Range	4.7 - 68.2	5.1 - 61.6	4.7 - 68.2
3	Mean	27.2	14.8	22.0
	Median	32.1	18.9	29.6
	Range	3.3 - 100.0	.3 - 40.0	.3 - 100.0
4	Mean	17.2	4.7	10.5
	Median	23.0	7.0	19.6
5	Circulation figures not given			
	Range	3.3 - 385.5	.3 - 75.8	.3 - 385.5
Total	Mean	23.6	18.4	19.5
	Median	27.8	16.9	23.3

These figures are based, as stated, on general stack circulation
divided by all borrowers recorded. But many, if not most, institutions have borrowers other than those recorded herein. Futhermore,
it is entirely possible that the larger institutions, or the private
institutions, have relatively more of these "other" borrowers than
do the smaller or public institutions. We do not know. It does
follow, however, that the presence of additional borrowers would
reduce per capita circulation given here.

V. LOAN PERIODS

A. Books

1. Faculty

Length of Loan	Category	Class 1	Class 2	Class 3	Class 4	Class 5	Total
Indefinite	Private	9 (69%)	10 (40%)	39 (39%)	49 (45%)	6 (23%)	113 (42%)
	Public	7 (33%)	11 (22%)	5 (15%)	20 (49%)	4 (36%)	47 (30%)
	Total	16 (47%)	21 (28%)	44 (33%)	69 (46%)	10 (27%)	160 (37%)
1 year or school year	Private	2 (16%)	3 (12%)	9 (9%)	8 (7%)	7 (27%)	29 (11%)
	Public	3 (14%)	10 (20%)	3 (9%)	1 (2%)	0	17 (11%)
	Total	5 (15%)	13 (17%)	12 (9%)	9 (6%)	7 (19%)	46 (11%)
6 months	Private	1 (8%)	1 (4%)	1 (1%)	0	0	3 (1%)
	Public	1 (5%)	1 (2%)	1 (3%)	0	0	3 (2%)
	Total	2 (6%)	2 (3%)	2 (2%)	0	0	6 (1%)
Semester or Quarter	Private	0	6 (24%)	19 (19%)	25 (23%)	8 (31%)	58 (21%)
	Public	5 (24%)	18 (36%)	17 (50%)	11 (27%)	2 (18%)	53 (34%)
	Total	5 (15%)	24 (32%)	36 (27%)	36 (24%)	10 (27%)	111 (26%)
3 months or $\frac{1}{2}$ semester	Private	0	1 (4%)	0	3 (3%)	0	4 (1%)
	Public	0	2 (4%)	0	0	1 (9%)	3 (2%)
	Total	0	3 (4%)	0	3 (2%)	1 (3%)	7 (2%)
7 weeks or 6 weeks	Private	0	0	2 (2%)	0	0	2 (1%)
	Public	0	0	0	0	0	0
	Total	0	0	2 (2%)	0	0	2 (-)
1 month, 30 days, or 4 weeks	Private	0	2 (8%)	14 (14%)	6 (6%)	3 (12%)	25 (9%)
	Public	1 (5%)	6 (12%)	4 (12%)	1 (2%)	1 (9%)	13 (8%)
	Total	1 (3%)	8 (11%)	18 (14%)	7 (5%)	4 (11%)	38 (9%)
3 weeks or 20 days	Private	0	1 (4%)	2 (2%)	1 (1%)	0	4 (1%)
	Public	1 (5%)	0	0	2 (5%)	1 (9%)	4 (3%)
	Total	1 (3%)	1 (1%)	2 (2%)	3 (2%)	1 (3%)	8 (2%)
2 weeks	Private	0	0	10 (10%)	12 (11%)	1 (4%)	23 (8%)
	Public	0	2 (4%)	3 (9%)	1 (2%)	1 (9%)	7 (4%)
	Total	0	2 (3%)	13 (10%)	13 (9%)	2 (6%)	30 (7%)
1 week	Private	0	0	0	0	0	0
	Public	0	0	0	2 (5%)	0	2 (1%)
	Total	0	0	0	2 (1%)	0	2 (-)

V. Loan Periods
   A. Books
      1. Faculty (Cont'd)

Length of Loan	Category	Class 1	Class 2	Class 3	Class 4	Class 5	Total
3 days	Private	0	0	0	1 (1%)	0	1 (-)
	Public	0	0	0	0	0	0
	Total	0	0	0	1 (1%)	0	1 (-)
non-circulating	Private	0	0	0	1 (1%)	0	1 (-)
	Public	0	0	0	0	0	0
	Total	0	0	0	1 (1%)	0	1 (-)
not given or not applicable	Private	1 (8%)	1 (4%)	2 (2%)	4 (4%)	3 (12%)	11 (4%)
	Public	1 (5%)	0	1 (3%)	3 (7%)	1 (9%)	6 (4%)
	Total	2 (6%)	1 (1%)	3 (2%)	7 (5%)	4 (11%)	17 (4%)

V. Loan Periods

   A. Books

     2. Graduate Students

Length of Loan	Category	Class 1	Class 2	Class 3	Class 4	Class 5	Total
indefinite	Private	0	0	0	1 (4%)	1 (11%)	2 (2%)
	Public	0	1 (2%)	0	1 (5%)	0	2 (2%)
	Total	0	1 (1%)	0	2 (4%)	1 (6%)	4 (2%)
school year	Private	0	0	1 (3%)	0	0	1 (1%)
	Public	0	0	0	0	0	0
	Total	0	0	1 (2%)	0	0	1 (-)
6 months	Private	0	0	0	0	0	0
	Public	0	0	1 (4%)	0	0	1 (1%)
	Total	0	0	1 (2%)	0	0	1 (-)
semester or quarter	Private	0	3 (13%)	1 (3%)	2 (8%)	1 (11%)	7 (6%)
	Public	2 (10%)	5 (11%)	1 (4%)	1 (5%)	2 (29%)	11 (9%)
	Total	2 (6%)	8 (11%)	2 (3%)	3 (7%)	3 (19%)	18 (8%)
3 months	Private	1 (8%)	0	0	0	0	1 (1%)
	Public	0	0	0	0	0	0
	Total	1 (3%)	0	0	0	0	1 (-)
1 month, 30 days or 4 weeks	Private	6 (46%)	7 (29%)	10 (25%)	7 (28%)	5 (56%)	35 (32%)
	Public	5 (25%)	16 (34%)	5 (21%)	4 (19%)	1 (14%)	31 (26%)
	Total	11 (33%)	23 (32%)	15 (24%)	11 (24%)	6 (38%)	66 (29%)
3 weeks	Private	2 (15%)	2 (8%)	7 (18%)	2 (8%)	1 (9%)	14 (13%)
	Public	3 (15%)	4 (9%)	2 (8%)	1 (5%)	1 (14%)	11 (9%)
	Total	5 (15%)	6 (9%)	9 (14%)	3 (7%)	2 (13%)	25 (11%)
2 weeks	Private	3 (22%)	11 (5%)	21 (52%)	12 (48%)	1 (11%)	48 (43%)
	Public	10 (50%)	19 (40%)	12 (50%)	8 (38%)	2 (29%)	51 (43%)
	Total	13 (39%)	30 (42%)	33 (52%)	20 (43%)	3 (19%)	99 (43%)
1 week	Private	0	0	1 (3%)	0	0	1 (1%)
	Public	0	0	0	4 (19%)	0	4 (3%)
	Total	0	0	1 (2%)	4 (9%)	0	5 (2%)

V. Loan Periods
   A. Books
      2. Graduate Students (Cont'd)

Length of Loan	Category	Class 1	Class 2	Class 3	Class 4	Class 5	Total
non-circulating	Private	0	0	0	1 (4%)	0	1 (1%)
	Public	0	0	0	0	0	0
	Total	0	0	0	1 (2%)	0	1 (-)
not given or not applicable	Private	1	2	56	82	17	158
	Public	0	5	13	22	5	45

1 Percentages are based on institutions which reported graduate enrollment. For this reason, percentages are not given in the category "not given or not applicable."

Percentages based on these figures:

Class	Private	Public	Total
1	13	20	33
2	24	47	71
3	40	24	64
4	25	21	46
5	9	7	16
total	111	119	230

12

V. Loan Periods

   A. Books

      3. Undergraduate Students

Length of Loan	Category	Class 1	Class 2	Class 3	Class 4	Class 5	Total
Indefinite	Private	0	0	0	1 (1%)	0	1 (-)
	Public	0	0	0	0	0	0
	Total	0	0	0	1 (1%)	0	1 (-)
6 months	Private	0	0	0	0	0	0
	Public	0	0	1 (3%)	0	0	1 (-)
	Total	0	0	1 (1%)	0	0	1 (-)
Semester or quarter	Private	0	1 (4%)	1 (1%)	0 (1%)	1 (4%)	3 (1%)
	Public	0	1 (2%)	2 (3%)	1 (2%)	0	4 (3%)
	Total	0	2 (3%)	3 (2%)	1 (1%)	1 (3%)	7 (2%)
3 months	Private	1 (8%)	0	0	0	0	1 (-)
	Public	0	0	0	0	0	0
	Total	1 (3%)	0	0	0	0	1 (-)
½ semester	Private	0	0	0	1 (1%)	0	1 (-)
	Public	0	0	0	0	0	0
	Total	0	0	0	1 (1%)	0	1 (-)
1 month, 30 days or 4 weeks	Private	5 (39%)	8 (32%)	14 (14%)	19 (18%)	6 (23%)	52 (19%)
	Public	1 (5%)	15 (30%)	3 (9%)	5 (12%)	2 (18%)	26 (17%)
	Total	6 (18%)	23 (31%)	17 (12%)	24 (17%)	8 (22%)	78 (18%)
3 weeks or 20 days	Private	2 (15%)	3 (12%)	18 (18%)	6 (6%)	5 (19%)	34 (13%)
	Public	5 (24%)	5 (10%)	2 (6%)	6 (15%)	1 (9%)	19 (12%)
	Total	7 (21%)	8 (11%)	20 (15%)	12 (8%)	6 (16%)	53 (13%)
2 weeks	Private	4 (31%)	14 (56%)	65 (66%)	72 (67%)	8 (30%)	163 (60%)
	Public	15 (71%)	27 (54%)	25 (73%)	20 (49%)	7 (64%)	94 (60%)
	Total	19 (56%)	41 (55%)	90 (68%)	92 (62%)	15 (41%)	257 (60%)
1 week	Private	0	0	1 (1%)	3 (3%)	2 (8%)	6 (2%)
	Public	0	0	0	4 (10%)	0	4 (3%)
	Total	0	0	1 (1%)	7 (5%)	2 (5%)	10 (2%)

V. Loan Periods

  A. Books

    3. Undergraduate Students (Cont'd)

Length of Loan	Category	Class 1	Class 2	Class 3	Class 4	Class 5	Total
Overnight	Private	0	0	0	0	0	0
	Public	0	0	0	1 (2%)	0	1 (-)
	Total	0	0	0	1 (1%)	0	1 (-)
non-circulating	Private	0	0	0	1 (1%)	0	1 (-)
	Public	0	0	0	0	0	0
	Total	0	0	0	1 (1%)	0	1 (-)
not given or not applicable	Private	1 (8%)	0	1 (1%)	4 (4%)	4 (15%)	6 (2%)
	Public	0	1 (2%)	1 (3%)	4 (10%)	1 (9%)	7 (4%)
	Total	1 (3%)	1 (1%)	2 (2%)	8 (5%)	5 (14%)	13 (3%)

Number of institutions reporting undergraduate enrollment. Percentages based on these figures:

Class	Private	Public	Total
1	13	21	34
2	25	50	75
3	99	34	133
4	107	41	148
5	26	11	37
Total	270	157	427

14

V. Loan Periods

   B. Periodicals

      1. Faculty

Length of Loan (condensed)	Category	Class 1	Class 2	Class 3	Class 4	Class 5	Total
Indefinite	Private	3 (23%)	0	19 (19%)	22 (20%)	3 (12%)	47 (17%)
	Public	2 (10%)	4 (8%)	5 (15%)	4 (10%)	3 (27%)	18 (11%)
	Total	5 (15%)	4 (5%)	24 (18%)	26 (17%)	6 (16%)	65 (15%)
1 quarter to 1 year	Private	1 (8%)	1 (4%)	2 (2%)	3 (3%)	2 (8%)	9 (3%)
	Public	1 (5%)	2 (4%)	2 (6%)	4 (10%)	0	9 (6%)
	Total	2 (6%)	3 (4%)	4 (3%)	7 (5%)	2 (6%)	18 (4%)
2 weeks to 6 weeks	Private	3 (23%)	2 (8%)	3 (3%)	11 (10%)	4 (15%)	23 (8%)
	Public	1 (5%)	4 (8%)	1 (3%)	3 (7%)	0	9 (6%)
	Total	4 (12%)	6 (8%)	4 (3%)	14 (9%)	4 (11%)	32 (7%)
5 days to 1 week	Private	2 (16%)	9 (36%)	11 (11%)	18 (16%)	2 (8%)	42 (15%)
	Public	3 (14%)	7 (14%)	2 (8%)	4 (10%)	1 (9%)	17 (11%)
	Total	5 (15%)	16 (21%)	13 (10%)	22 (15%)	3 (8%)	59 (14%)
1 day to 3 days	Private	0	2 (8%)	12 (12%)	14 (13%)	5 (19%)	33 (12%)
	Public	4 (20%)	6 (12%)	4 (12%)	4 (10%)	1 (9%)	19 (12%)
	Total	4 (12%)	8 (11%)	16 (12%)	18 (12%)	6 (16%)	52 (12%)
2 hours to overnight	Private	0	5 (20%)	17 (17%)	19 (17%)	2 (8%)	43 (15%)
	Public	4 (19%)	8 (16%)	11 (32%)	6 (15%)	4 (36%)	33 (21%)
	Total	4 (12%)	13 (17%)	28 (21%)	25 (17%)	6 (16%)	76 (18%)
do not circulate	Private	2 (16%)	6 (24%)	26 (26%)	16 (15%)	4 (15%)	54 (20%)
	Public	6 (29%)	17 (34%)	7 (21%)	12 (30%)	2 (18%)	44 (28%)
	Total	8 (24%)	23 (31%)	33 (25%)	28 (119%)	6 (16%)	98 (23%)
not given	Private	2 (16%)	0	9 (9%)	6 (6%)	4 (15%)	21 (8%)
	Public	0	2 (4%)	2 (8%)	4 (10%)	0	8 (5%)
	Total	2 (6%)	2 (3%)	11 (8%)	10 (7%)	4 (11%)	29 (7%)

V. Loan Periods

    B. Periodicals

        2. Graduate Students[1]

Length of Loan (condensed)	Category	Class 1	Class 2	Class 3	Class 4	Class 5	Total
Indefinite	Private	0	0	0	0	1 (11%)	1 (1%)
	Public	0	0	0	0	0	0
	Total	0	0	0	0	1 (2%)	1 (-)
1 quarter to 1 year	Private	0	0	0	1 (4%)	1 (11%)	2 (2%)
	Public	0	0	2 (8%)	0	1 (14%)	3 (3%)
	Total	0	0	2 (3%)	1 (2%)	2 (13%)	5 (2%)
2 weeks to 6 weeks	Private	2 (16%)	0	1 (3%)	2 (8%)	0	5 (4%)
	Public	1 (5%)	2 (4%)	0	2 (10%)	0	5 (4%)
	Total	3 (9%)	2 (3%)	1 (2%)	4 (8%)	0	10 (4%)
5 days to 1 week	Private	3 (23%)	4 (17%)	2 (5%)	3 (12%)	0	12 (11%)
	Public	1 (5%)	2 (4%)	1 (4%)	3 (14%)	0	7 (6%)
	Total	4 (12%)	6 (9%)	3 (5%)	6 (13%)	0	19 (9%)
1 day to 3 days	Private	0	1 (4%)	2 (5%)	2 (8%)	2 (22%)	7 (6%)
	Public	2 (10%)	5 (11%)	1 (4%)	1 (5%)	2 (29%)	11 (9%)
	Total	2 (6%)	6 (8%)	3 (5%)	3 (7%)	4 (25%)	18 (8%)
2 hours to overnight	Private	1 (8%)	3 (12%)	7 (18%)	2 (8%)	0	13 (12%)
	Public	3 (15%)	9 (19%)	5 (21%)	3 (14%)	0	20 (17%)
	Total	4 (12%)	12 (17%)	12 (19%)	5 (11%)	0	33 (14%)
do not circulate	Private	6 (46%)	13 (54%)	27 (68%)	14 (56%)	4 (44%)	64 (58%)
	Public	14 (70%)	25 (53%)	12 (50%)	9 (43%)	3 (43%)	63 (53%)
	Total	20 (63%)	38 (54%)	39 (61%)	23 (50%)	7 (44%)	127 (55%)
not given, or not applicable	Private	1	4	60	85	18	168
	Public	0	7	13	23	5	48

1 Percentages based on figures given on page 12.

V. Loan Periods

   B. Periodicals

      3. Undergraduate Students[1]

Length of Loan (condensed)	Category	Class 1	Class 2	Class 3	Class 4	Class 5	Total
Indefinite	Private	0	0	0	2 (2%)	0	2 (1%)
	Public	0	0	0	0	0	0
	Total	0	0	0	2 (1%)	0	2 (-)
1 quarter to 1 year	Private	0	0	1 (1%)	0	1 (4%)	2 (1%)
	Public	0	0	2 (6%)	0	0	2 (1%)
	Total	0	0	3 (2%)	0	1 (3%)	4 (1%)
2 weeks to 6 weeks	Private	2 (16%)	1 (4%)	2 (2%)	6 (6%)	1 (4%)	12 (4%)
	Public	1 (5%)	1 (2%)	0	2 (5%)	1 (9%)	5 (3%)
	Total	3 (9%)	2 (3%)	2 (2%)	8 (5%)	2 (5%)	17 (4%)
5 days to 1 week	Private	1 (8%)	2 (8%)	6 (6%)	10 (9%)	1 (4%)	20 (7%)
	Public	0	0	1 (3%)	3 (7%)	2 (18%)	11 (7%)
	Total	1 (3%)	2 (3%)	7 (5%)	13 (9%)	3 (8%)	31 (7%)
1 day to 3 days	Private	0	2 (8%)	7 (7%)	12 (11%)	2 (8%)	23 (9%)
	Public	0	4 (8%)	0	6 (15%)	1 (9%)	11 (7%)
	Total	0	6 (8%)	7 (5%)	18 (12%)	3 (8%)	34 (8%)
2 hours to overnight	Private	0	5 (20%)	17 (17%)	19 (18%)	3 (12%)	44 (16%)
	Public	4 (19%)	10 (20%)	9 (26%)	5 (12%)	2 (18%)	30 (19%)
	Total	4 (12%)	15 (20%)	26 (20%)	24 (16%)	5 (14%)	74 (17%)
do not circulate	Private	9 (69%)	9 (36%)	54 (55%)	49 (46%)	12 (46%)	133 (49%)
	Public	16 (76%)	30 (60%)	16 (46%)	20 (49%)	4 (36%)	86 (55%)
	Total	25 (74%)	39 (52%)	70 (53%)	69 (47%)	16 (43%)	219 (51%)
not given or not applicable	Private	1	6	12	11	6	36
	Public	0	5	6	5	1	17
	Total	1	11	18	16	7	53

[1] Percentages based on figures given on page 14.

17

V. Loan Periods

   C. Pamphlets

The majority of academic libraries do not distinguish between books and pamphlet material, except, perhaps, with regard to so-called vertical file material. In the great majority of cases, the person filling out the questionnaire simply wrote in the section for pamphlets "same as books."

This section should have been omitted from the academic part of the questionnaire. Not only are pamphlets treated as books in most cases, but the question also led to some confusion, because several librarians did not know what was meant by pamphlets.

For these reasons, no summary of pamphlet loans will be given.

V. Loan Periods

D. Reserve Books

Loan periods for reserve books are based on the nature of the
material and not on the status of the borrower; therefore will
not be a breakdown of reserve loans by type of borrower.

The 429 institutions surveyed indicated no fewer than 39 different combinations of reserve loan periods. It would be interesting
to know how many there are altogether. Doubtless each institution
that has several combinations has its reasons, but one cannot help
but wonder if institutions maintaining three, four and even five
different loan periods for reserve books are not seeking complexi-
ty for its own sake.

Length of Loan	Category	Class 1	Class 2	Class 3	Class 4	Class 5	Total
do not circulate	Private	1 (8%)	0	2 (2%)	5 (5%)	1 (4%)	9 (3%)
	Public	1 (5%)	0	1 (3%)	2 (5%)	0	4 (3%)
	Total	2 (6%)	0	3 (2%)	7 (5%)	1 (3%)	13 (3%)
overnight only	Private	3 (23%)	4 (16%)	39 (39%)	55 (50%)	7 (27%)	109 (40%)
	Public	3 (14%)	4 (8%)	12 (35%)	8 (20%)	5 (45%)	46 (29%)
	Total	6 (18%)	8 (11%)	51 (38%)	63 (42%)	12 (32%)	155 (36%)
both overnight and 1 day books	Private	2 (16%)	1 (4%)	3 (3%)	7 (7%)	0	13 (5%)
	Public	1 (5%)	1 (2%)	2 (6%)	1 (2%)	0	5 (3%)
	Total	3 (9%)	2 (3%)	5 (4%)	8 (5%)	0	18 (4%)
overnight and 3 day books	Private	0	0	12 (12%)	5 (5%)	7 (27%)	24 (9%)
	Public	4 (19%)	2 (4%)	3 (9%)	2 (5%)	0	11 (7%)
	Total	4 (12%)	2 (3%)	15 (11%)	7 (5%)	7 (9%)	35 (8%)
overnight and 5 day books	Private	0	0	1 (1%)	2 (2%)	0	3 (1%)
	Public	0	1 (2%)	0	0	0	1 (-)
	Total	0	1 (1%)	1 (1%)	2 (1%)	0	4 (1%)
overnight and 7 day books	Private	0	1 (4%)	3 (3%)	3 (3%)	0	7 (3%)
	Public	1 (5%)	2 (4%)	1 (3%)	6 (15%)	0	10 (6%)
	Total	1 (3%)	3 (4%)	4 (3%)	9 (6%)	0	17 (4%)
overnight and 14 day books	Private	0	0	1 (1%)	0	0	1 (-)
	Public	0	1 (2%)	0	0	0	1 (-)
	Total	0	1 (1%)	1 (1%)	0	0	2 (-)

V. Loan Periods

D. Reserve Books (Cont'd)

Length of Loan	Category	Class 1	Class 2	Class 3	Class 4	Class 5	Total
overnight, 1 and 2 day books	Private	0	1 (4%)	2 (2%)	0	0	3 (1%)
	Public	0	0	0	0	0	0
	Total	0	1 (1%)	2 (2%)	0	0	3 (1%)
overnight, 1 and 3 day books	Private	0	3 (12%)	4 (4%)	5 (5%)	0	12 (4%)
	Public	0	2 (4%)	1 (3%)	2 (5%)	1 (9%)	6 (4%)
	Total	0	5 (7%)	5 (4%)	7 (5%)	1 (3%)	18 (4%)
overnight, 1 and 5 day books	Private	0	1 (4%)	1 (1%)	1 (1%)	0	3 (1%)
	Public	0	0	1 (3%)	1 (2%)	0	2 (1%)
	Total	0	1 (1%)	2 (1%)	2 (1%)	0	5 (1%)
overnight, 1 and 7 day books	Private	0	1 (4%)	4 (4%)	2 (2%)	0	7 (3%)
	Public	0	2 (4%)	2 (6%)	1 (2%)	1 (9%)	6 (4%)
	Total	0	3 (4%)	6 (4%)	3 (2%)	1 (3%)	13 (3%)
overnight, 2 and 3 day books	Private	0	0	0	0	0	0
	Public	0	1 (2%)	1 (3%)	0	0	2 (1%)
	Total	0	1 (1%)	1 (1%)	0	0	2 (-)
overnight, 2 and 7 day books	Private	0	1 (4%)	0	0	0	1 (-)
	Public	1 (5%)	1 (2%)	1 (3%)	1 (2%)	0	4 (3%)
	Total	1 (3%)	2 (3%)	1 (1%)	1 (1%)	0	5 (1%)
overnight, 3 and 7 day books	Private	0	2 (8%)	5 (5%)	3 (3%)	1 (4%)	11 (4%)
	Public	1 (5%)	6 (12%)	2 (6%)	5 (12%)	0	14 (9%)
	Total	1 (3%)	8 (11%)	7 (5%)	8 (5%)	1 (3%)	25 (6%)
overnight, 5 and 7 day books*	Private	0	0	0	0	0	0
	Public	1 (5%)	0	0	0	0	1 (1%)
	Total	1 (3%)	0	0	0	0	1 (-)
overnight, 7 and 14 day books	Private	0	0	0	1 (1%)	0	1 (-)
	Public	0	0	0	0	0	0
	Total	0	0	0	1 (1%)	0	1 (-)

D. Reserve Books (Cont'd)

Length of Loan	Category	Class 1	Class 2	Class 3	Class 4	Class 5	Total
overnight, 1, 2 and 3 day books	Private	0	0	0	1 (1%)	0	1 (-)
	Public	0	0	0	0	0	0
	Total	0	0	0	1 (1%)	0	1 (-)
overnight, 1, 2 and 7 day books	Private	0	1 (4%)	2 (2%)	1 (1%)	0	4 (1%)
	Public	0	1 (2%)	0	0	0	1 (1%)
	Total	0	2 (3%)	2 (2%)	1 (1%)	0	5 (1%)
overnight`1, 3 and 7 day books	Private	3 (23%)	0	4 (4%)	2 (2%)	1 (4%)	10 (4%)
	Public	2 (10%)	3 (6%)	0	0	0	5 (3%)
	Total	5 (15%)	3 (4%)	4 (3%)	2 (1%)	1 (3%)	15 (4%)
overnight, 1, 5 and 7 day books	Private	0	0	0	1 (1%)	0	1 (-)
	Public	0	1 (2%)	0	2 (6%)	0	3 (2%)
	Total	0	1 (1%)	0	3 (2%)	0	4 (1%)
overnight, 1, 7 and 14 day books	Private	0	1 (4%)	0	0	0	1 (-)
	Public	0	0	2 (6%)	0	0	2 (1%)
	Total	0	1 (1%)	2 (2%)	0	0	3 (1%)
overnight, 3, 7 and 14 day books	Private	0	0	0	0	0	0
	Public	0	0	0	1 (3%)	0	1 (-)
	Total	0	0	0	1 (1%)	0	1 (-)
overnight, 1, 2, 3, and 7 day books	Private	0	0	1 (1%)	0	0	1 (-)
	Public	0	0	0	0	0	0
	Total	0	0	1 (1%)	0	0	1 (-)
overnight, 1, 2,4 and 7 day books	Private	0	0	0	0	0	0
	Public	1 (5%)	0	0	0	0	1 (1%)
	Total	1 (3%)	0	0	0	0	1 (-)
overnight, 1, 3, 5, and 7 day books	Private	0	0	0	0	0	0
	Public	0	0	1 (3%)	0	0	1 (1%)
	Total	0	0	1 (1%)	0	0	1 (-)
overnight, 1, 3, 7 and 14 day books	Private	0	0	1 (1%)	0	0	1 (-)
	Public	0	2 (4%)	1 (3%)	0	0	3 (2%)
	Total	0	2 (3%)	2 (2%)	0	0	4 (1%)

V. Loan Periods

    D. Reserve Books (Cont'd)

Length of Loan	Category	Class 1	Class 2	Class 3	Class 4	Class 5	Total
overnight, 3, 5, 7 and 14 day books	Private	1 (8%)	0	0	0	0	1 (-)
	Public	0	0	0	0	0	0
	Total	1 (3%)	0	0	0	0	1 (-)
1 day books	Private	0	0	2 (2%)	1 (1%)	0	3 (1%)
	Public	0	0	0	0	0	0
	Total	0	0	2 (2%)	1 (1%)	0	3 (1%)
2 day books	Private	0	0	0	1 (1%)	0	1 (-)
	Public	0	0	0	0	0	0
	Total	0	0	0	1 (1%)	0	1 (-)
Weekend books[1]	Private	0	0	0	0	0	0
	Public	0	0	0	1 (2%)	0	1 (1%)
	Total	0	0	0	1 (1%)	0	1 (-)
3 day books	Private	0	1 (4%)	0	1 (1%)	0	2 (1%)
	Public	3 (14%)	1 (2%)	0	0	1 (9%)	5 (3%)
	Total	3 (9%)	2 (3%)	0	1 (1%)	1 (1%)	7 (2%)
14 day books	Private	0	0	0	1 (1%)	0	1 (-)
	Public	0	0	0	0	0	0
	Total	0	0	0	1 (1%)	0	1 (-)
1 and 3 day books	Private	0	1 (4%)	0	0	3 (12%)	4 (1%)
	Public	1 (5%)	1 (2%)	0	0	0	2 (1%)
	Total	1 (3%)	2 (3%)	0	0	3 (9%)	6 (1%)
1 and 7 day books	Private	0	0	1 (1%)	0	0	1 (-)
	Public	0	0	0	0	0	0
	Total	0	0	1 (1%)	0	0	1 (-)
2 and 7 day books	Private	0	0	0	0	0	0
	Public	1 (5%)	0	0	1 (2%)	0	2 (1%)
	Total	1 (3%)	0	0	1 (1%)	0	2 (-)

V. Loan Periods

   D. Reserve Books (Cont'd)

Length of Loan	Category	Class 1	Class 2	Class 3	Class 4	Class 5	Total
1, 3 and 7 day books	Private	1 (8%)	1 (4%)	0	0	0	2 (-)
	Public	0	0	0	0	0	0
	Total	1 (3%)	1 (1%)	0	0	0	2 (-)
2, 3 and 7 day books	Private	0	0	0	0	0	0
	Public	0	1 (2%)	0	0	0	1 (1%)
	Total	0	1 (1%)	0	0	0	1 (-)
not applicable	Private	0	0	0	2 (2%)	1 (1%)	3 (1%)
	Public	0	0	0	2 (5%)	1 (9%)	3 (2%)
	Total	0	0	0	4 (3%)	2 (5%)	6 (1%)
not specific	Private	0	0	1	1	1	3
	Public	0	0	1	1	0	2
	Total	0	0	2	2	1	5
not given	Private	2	5	10	8	4	29
	Public	0	3	2	4	2	11
	Total	2	8	12	12	6	40

V. Loan Periods

   E. General

      1. Materials over which circulation control is maintained

        a. Range - - - non-circulating - forever[2]

        b. Total number of possible loan periods, all materials and all borrowers

indefinite	6 weeks	4 days
1 year	1 month	3 days
school year	30 days	weekend
6 months	4 weeks	2 days
semester	3 weeks	1 day
quarter	20 days	overnight
3 months	2 weeks	3 hours
½ semester	1 week	2 hours
7 weeks	5 days	non-circulating

23

1 Loan period(s) Monday-Thursday not mentioned.

2 Answer given by one librarian regarding loans to faculty.

VI. RENEWALS

A. By telephone

| Class | Category | Type of Material[1] | | | | | |
| | | Books | | Periodicals | | Reserve | |
		YES	NO	YES	NO	YES	NO
1	Private	4 (31%)[2]	9 (69%)	3 (25%)	9 (75%)	1 (9%)	11 (91%)
	Public	3 (15%)	17 (85%)	2 (13%)	14 (87%)	0	19 (100%)
	Total	7 (21%)	26 (79%)	5 (18%)	23 (82%)	1 (3%)	30 (97%)
2	Private	8 (35%)	15 (65%)	0	19 (100%)	7 (30%)	16 (70%)
	Public	6 (13%)	42 (87%)	4 (10%)	38 (90%)	3 (6%)	47 (94%)
	Total	14 (20%)	57 (80%)	4 (7%)	57 (93%)	10 (14%)	63 (86%)
3	Private	46 (47%)	51 (53%)	18 (26%)	51 (74%)	10 (11%)	82 (89%)
	Public	14 (42%)	19 (58%)	5 (17%)	25 (83%)	3 (9%)	31 (91%)
	Total	60 (46%)	70 (54%)	23 (23%)	76 (77%)	13 (10%)	113 (90%)
4	Private	53 (52%)	48 (48%)	11 (13%)	72 (87%)	8 (8%)	90 (92%)
	Public	19 (54%)	16 (46%)	9 (33%)	18 (67%)	6 (18%)	28 (82%)
	Total	72 (53%)	64 (47%)	20 (18%)	90 (82%)	14 (11%)	118 (89%)
5	Private	9 (38%)	15 (62%)	2 (10%)	19 (90%)	3 (13%)	20 (87%)
	Public	3 (30%)	7 (70%)	3 (30%)	7 (70%)	3 (27%)	8 (73%)
	Total	12 (35%)	22 (65%)	5 (16%)	26 (84%)	6 (18%)	28 (82%)
Total	Private	120 (46%)	138 (54%)	34 (17%)	170 (83%)	29 (12%)	219 (88%)
	Public	45 (31%)	101 (69%)	23 (18%)	102 (82%)	15 (10%)	133 (90%)
	Total	165 (41%)	239 (59%)	57 (17%)	272 (83%)	44 (11%)	352 (89%)

1 Pamphlets excluded.

2 Percentages based on libraries reporting. Not given and not applicable
excluded from all types for uniformity.

VI. Renewals

  B. With book in hand

| Class | Category | Type of Material[1] | | | | | | |
| | | Books | | Periodicals | | Reserve | |
		YES	NO	YES	NO	YES	NO
1	Private	9 (100%)[1]	0	7 (78%)	3 (22%)	6 (55%)	4 (45%)
	Public	21 (100%)	0	8 (57%)	6 (43%)	13 (65%)	7 (35%)
	Total	30 (100%)	0	15 (63%)	9 (37%)	19 (61%)	12 (39%)
2	Private	21 (87%)	3 (13%)	9 (50%)	9 (50%)	14 (61%)	9 (39%)
	Public	45 (92%)	4 (8%)	17 (40%)	25 (60%)	20 (42%)	28 (58%)
	Total	66 (90%)	7 (10%)	26 (43%)	34 (57%)	34 (48%)	37 (52%)
3	Private	82 (86%)	13 (14%)	33 (48%)	36 (52%)	43 (49%)	45 (51%)
	Public	29 (85%)	5 (15%)	11 (37%)	19 (63%)	18 (49%)	19 (51%)
	Total	111 (86%)	18 (14%)	44 (44%)	55 (56%)	61 (49%)	63 (51%)
4	Private	105 (99%)	1 (1%)	50 (59%)	35 (41%)	57 (56%)	44 (44%)
	Public	35 (97%)	1 (3%)	17 (68%)	8 (32%)	20 (56%)	16 (44%)
	Total	140 (99%)	2 (1%)	67 (61%)	43 (39%)	77 (56%)	60 (44%)
5	Private	23 (88%)	3 (12%)	8 (35%)	14 (65%)	10 (40%)	15 (60%)
	Public	8 (88%)	1 (12%)	5 (55%)	4 (45%)	6 (55%)	5 (45%)
	Total	31 (88%)	4 (12%)	13 (42%)	18 (58%)	16 (44%)	20 (56%)
Total	Private	240 (92%)	20 (8%)	107 (52%)	97 (48%)	130 (52%)	118 (48%)
	Public	138 (93%)	11 (7%)	58 (48%)	62 (52%)	77 (51%)	75 (49%)
	Total	378 (92%)	31 (8%)	165 (51%)	159 (49%)	207 (52%)	193 (48%)

1 Pamphlets excluded.

2 Percentages based on libraries reporting. Not given and not applicable
  excluded from all types for uniformity.

VII. OVERDUE CORRESPONDENCE

   A. Type of notice

      1. Class 1

Type of Notice	Category	1st	2nd	3rd	4th	5th
written	Private	12 (92%)	7	2	0	0
	Public	19 (90%)	11	7	2	0
	Total	31 (90%)	18	9	2	0
bill (written)	Private	0	3	1	1	0
	Public	0	2	2	2	0
	Total	0	5	3	3	0
telephone	Private	0	0	1	0	0
	Public	1 (5%)	0	1	0	0
	Total	1 (3%)	0	2	0	0
written and/or telephone	Private	1 (8%)	0	1	0	0
	Public	0	0	0	0	0
	Total	1 (3%)	0	1	0	0
university[2] official	Private	0	1	1	1	1
	Public	1 (5%)	4	1	1	1
	Total	1 (3%)	5	2	2	2
faculty advisor	Private	0	0	0	1	0
	Public	0	0	0	0	0
	Total	0	0	0	1	0

Number of institutions that send:

Number	Private	Public	Total
1 notice only	2 (16%)	4 (19%)	6 (18%)
2 notices	5 (39%)	6 (29%)	11 (32%)
3 notices	3 (23%)	7 (33%)	10 (29%)
4 notices	2 (16%)	3 (14%)	5 (15%)
5 notices	1 (8%)	1 (5%)	2 (6%)

1 Percentages given for first notice only. Percentages based on declining numbers
would be, in this application, confusing, as well as meaningless.

2 Dean, registrar, or bursar.

VII. Overdue Correspondence
  A. Type of notice
    2. Class 2

Type of Notice	Category	1st	2nd	3rd	4th	5th
written	Private	23 (92%)	20	11	2	0
	Public	48 (96%)	37	21	9	0
	Total	71 (95%)	57	32	11	0
bill (written)	Private	0	3	2	0	0
	Public	0	4	2	0	0
	Total	0	7	4	0	0
telephone	Private	1 (4%)	0	0	1	0
	Public	2 (4%)	1	4	2	1
	Total	3 (4%)	1	4	3	1
written and/or telephone	Private	1 (4%)	0	0	0	0
	Public	0	0	0	0	0
	Total	1 (1%)	0	0	0	0
university official	Private	0	1	5	5	0
	Public	0	4	7	3	4
	Total	0	5	12	8	4
faculty advisor	Private	0	1	0	0	0
	Public	0	0	0	0	0
	Total	0	1	0	0	0

Number of institutions that send:

Number	Private	Public	Total
1 notice only	0	4 (8%)	4 (5%)
2 notices	7 (28%)	12 (24%)	19 (25%)
3 notices	10 (40%)	20 (40%)	30 (40%)
4 notices	8 (32%)	9 (18%)	17 (23%)
5 notices	0	5 (10%)	5 (7%)

VII. Overdue Correspondence

    A. Type of notice

        3. Class 3

Type of Notice	Category	1st	2nd	3rd	4th	5th
written	Private	83 (84%)	75	55[1]	15	1
	Public	31 (91%)	28	17	3	0
	Total	114 (86%)	103	72	18	1
bill (written)	Private	0	3	2	5	2
	Public	0	1	1	2	0
	Total	0	4	3	7	2
telephone	Private	2 (2%)	2	9	4	0
	Public	0	2	4	3[2]	0
	Total	2 (2%)	4	13	7	0
written and/or telephone	Private	5 (5%)	4	2	0	0
	Public	0	0	1	0	0
	Total	5 (4%)	4	3	0	0
messenger	Private	2 (2%)	0	1	1	0
	Public	0	0	0	0	1
	Total	2 (2%)	0	1	1	1
posted list	Private	3 (3%)	2	1	0	0
	Public	0	0	0	1	0
	Total	3 (2%)	2	1	1	0
university official	Private	0	5	9	27	6
	Public	0	1	4	12	5
	Total	0	6	13	39	11
faculty advisor	Private	0	2	0	0	0
	Public	0	1	1	0	0
	Total	0	3	1	0	0
student government	Private	0	1	0	2	0
	Public	0	0	0	0	0
	Total	0	1	0	2	0

[1] In three cases, the notice is from a library official, either the head librarian, or the head of the circulation department.

28

VII.   Overdue Correspondence
  A.   Type of notice
      3. Class 3 (Cont'd)

2 In one case, the notice is from the head librarian.

Number of libraries that send:

Number	Private	Public	Total
1 notice only	3 (3%)	0	3 (2%)
2 notices	15 (15%)	5 (15%)	20 (15%)
3 notices	21 (21%)	7 (21%)	28 (21%)
4 notices	47 (47%)	15 (44%)	62 (47%)
5 notices	9 (9%)	5 (15%)	14 (11%)

VII. Overdue Correspondence

  A. Type of notice

    4. Class 4

Type of Notice	Category	1st	2nd	3rd	4th	5th
written	Private	97 (89%)	87	60	17	1
	Public	32 (78%)	27	22	6	0
	Total	129 (86%)	114	82	23	1
bill (written)	Private	0	1	4	2	1
	Public	0	3	0	0	1
	Total	0	4	4	2	2
telephone	Private	0	4	6	13	0
	Public	2 (5%)	2	2	2	0
	Total	2 (2%)	6	8	15	0
written and/or telephone	Private	3 (3%)	4	4	2	0
	Public	1 (2%)	0	0	0	0
	Total	4 (3%)	4	4	2	0
messenger	Private	2 (2%)	1	1	3	1
	Public	0	0	0	0	0
	Total	2 (2%)	1	1	3	1
posted list	Private	4 (4%)	1	2	1	1
	Public	3 (7%)	1	0	0	0
	Total	7 (5%)	2	2	1	1
university official	Private	0	0	11	25	15
	Public	0	1	4	8	6[1]
	Total	0	1	15	33	21
faculty advisor	Private	1 (1%)	0	1	1	0
	Public	0	0	0	0	0
	Total	1 (1%)	0	1	1	0
student government	Private	0	3	0	0	0
	Public	0	0	0	0	0
	Total	0	3	0	0	0

1 In one case, the notice represents formal notification of suspension; in one other, it represents notification that the student has been reported to a state official.

VII. Overdue Correspondence

    A. Type of notice

        4. Class 4 (Cont'd)

Number of institutions that send:

Number	Private	Public	Total
1 notice only	5 (5%)	4 (19%)	9 (6%)
2 notices	11 (11%)	7 (17%)	18 (12%)
3 notices	25 (23%)	12 (29%)	37 (25%)
4 notices	46 (42%)	10 (24%)	56 (37%)
5 notices	18 (16%)	5 (12%)	23 (15%)
none	2 (2%)	0	2 (1%)

VII. Overdue Correspondence

    A. Type of notice

        5. Class 5

Type of Notice	Category	1st	2nd	3rd	4th	5th
written	Private	23 (89%)	19	14	1	0
	Public	11 (100%)	10	6	1	0
	Total	34 (92%)	29	20	2	0
bill (written)	Private	0	0	1	1	0
	Public	0	0	0	1	1
	Total	0	0	1	2	1
telephone	Private	0	1	1	1	0
	Public	0	0	0	1	0
	Total	0	1	1	2	0
posted list	Private	0	1	1	0	0
	Public	0	0	0	0	0
	Total	0	1	1	0	0
university official	Private	0	1	1	8	1
	Public	0	0	2	1	0
	Total	0	1	3	9	1

Number of institutions that send:

Number	Private	Public	Total
1 notice only	1 (4%)	1 (9%)	2 (5%)

31

VII. Overdue Correspondence
   A. Type of notice
      5. Class 5 (Cont'd)

Number	Private	Public	Total
2 notices	4 (15%)	2 (18%)	6 (16%)
3 notices	7 (27%)	3 (27%)	10 (27%)
4 notices	9 (35%)	3 (27%)	12 (32%)
5 notices	1 (4%)	1 (9%)	2 (5%)
none	1 (4%)	0	1 (3%)

VII. Overdue Correspondence
   A. Type of notice
      6. All libraries

Type of Notice	Category	1st	2nd	3rd	4th	5th
written	Private	238 (87%)	203	142	35	2
	Public	141 (90%)	75	73	21	0
	Total	379 (88%)	278	215	56	2
bill (written)	Private	0	10	10	9	3
	Public	0	10	5	5	2
	Total	0	20	15	14	5
telephone	Private	3 (1%)	7	17	19	0
	Public	5 (3%)	5	11	8	1
	Total	8 (2%)	12	28	27	1
written and/or telephone	Private	10 (4%)	8	7	2	0
	Public	1 (1%)	0	1	0	0
	Total	11 (3%)	8	8	2	0
messenger	Private	4 (1%)	1	2	4	0
	Public	0	0	0	0	1
	Total	4 (1%)	1	2	4	1
posted list	Private	7 (3%)	4	4	1	1
	Public	3 (2%)	1	0	1	0
	Total	10 (2%)	5	4	2	1
university official	Private	0	8	27	66	23
	Public	1 (1%)	10	18	25	16
	Total	1 (-)	18	45	91	39

VII. Overdue Correspondence

   A. Type of notice

      6. All libraries (Cont'd)

Type of Notice	Category	1st	2nd	3rd	4th	5th
faculty advisor	Private	1 (-)	3	1	2	0
	Public	0	1	1	0	0
	Total	1 (-)	4	2	2	0
student government	Private	0	4	0	2	0
	Public	0	0	0	0	0
	Total	0	4	0	2	0

Number of institutions that send:

Number	Private	Public	Total
1 notice only	11 (4%)	13 (8%)	24 (6%)
2 notices	42 (15%)	32 (20%)	74 (17%)
3 notices	66 (24%)	49 (31%)	115 (27%)
4 notices	112 (42%)	40 (25%)	152 (36%)
5 notices	29 (11%)	17 (11%)	46 (11%)
none	3 (1%)	0	3 (1%)
not given	9 (3%)	6 (4%)	15 (3%)

VII. OVERDUE CORRESPONDENCE

B. Interval between notices

1. Class 1

The information below is in condensed form. Intervals between notices varied
remarkably from library to library. There were, in fact, a total of 55 different intervals, ranging from 1 day to "as time permits." Comparable intervals
were grouped, thus avoiding the problem of having too many intervals represented
by only one library. For example, the intervals 4 days, 4 to 5 days, 3 to 5
days, 1 to 7 days, and 1 to 6 days were combined under 4 days.

Variation in intervals between notices among academic libraries is not only
remarkable, it is truly amazing. The time lapse between when a book becomes
overdue and the first notice is sent, for example, may be anywhere from 1 to
183 days.

Percentages are given only for intervals between when a book becomes overdue
and the first notice is sent. This was done for several reasons. First, was
the declining numbers in columns two to five (1st to 2nd notice, 2nd to 3rd,
etc.) It seemed pointless to indicate a percentage for a library that waited
two weeks between the 4th and 5th notice, when, in fact, only one library might
do this. 100% of a field of 1 doesn't mean a great deal. But second, and more
important, was the fact that few libraries seemed to employ regular intervals.
The final notice, for example, be it second, third, fourth or fifth, was fre-
quently sent near the end of the semester. Libraries that waited 1 or 2 weeks
before sending the first notice were more prone to send succeeding notices at
1 or 2 week intervals. Libraries that sent the first notice the day after the
book became overdue waited longer, of course, before sending the 2nd, 3rd, etc.
This accounts for the higher numbers of the 2nd notices than the 1st in certain
intervals.

Interval	Category	Overdue & 1st	1st & 2nd	2nd & 3rd	3rd & 4th	4th & 5th
3 days	Private	1 (8%)	1	1	0	0
	Public	2 (10%)	0	0	0	0
	Total	3 (9%)	1	1	0	0
4 days	Private	0	0	0	0	0
	Public	3 (14%)	0	0	0	0
	Total	3 (9%)	0	0	0	0
5 days	Private	3 (24%)	0	0	0	0
	Public	1 (5%)	0	0	0	0
	Total	4 (12%)	0	0	0	0
7 days	Private	4 (31%)	2	1	0	0
	Public	5 (24%)	7	3	0	0
	Total	9 (26%)	9	4	0	0

VII. Overdue Correspondence
   B. Interval between notices
      1. Class 1 (Cont'd)

Interval	Category	Overdue & 1st	1st & 2nd	2nd & 3rd	3rd & 4th	4th & 5th
8 days	Private	1 (8%)	1	1	0	0
	Public	1 (5%)	0	1	0	0
	Total	2 (6%)	1	2	0	0
10 days	Private	0	0	1	0	0
	Public	1 (5%)	1	1	0	0
	Total	1 (3%)	1	2	0	0
2 weeks	Private	0	3	0	0	0
	Public	6 (29%)	1	4	2	1
	Total	6 (9%)	4	4	2	1
3 weeks	Private	0	0	0	0	0
	Public	0	2	0	0	0
	Total	0	2	0	0	0
1 month	Private	2 (16%)	0	0	0	0
	Public	1 (5%)	3	1	1	0
	Total	3 (9%)	3	1	1	0
5 weeks	Private	0	0	0	0	0
	Public	0	1	1	0	0
	Total	0	1	1	0	0
8 weeks	Private	0	1	0	0	0
	Public	0	0	0	0	0
	Total	0	1	0	0	0
end of semester	Private	0	0	1	0	0
	Public	0	1	0	0	0
	Total	0	1	1	0	0
varies[1]	Private	1 (8%)	1	0	0	0
	Public	1 (5%)	0	0	0	0
	Total	2 (6%)	1	0	0	0

VII. Overdue Correspondence

    B. Interval between notices

        1. Class 1 (Cont'd)

Interval	Category	Overdue & 1st	1st & 2nd	2nd & 3rd	3rd & 4th	4th & 5th
not given, or not applicable	Private	1	4	8	13	13
	Public	0	5	10	18	20
	Total[2]	1	9	18	31	33

1 Varies, irregular, as time permits

2 Figures here, particularly after 1st-2nd, are high because of the number of institutions that do not send 3rd, 4th and 5th notices.

VII. Overdue Correspondence

    B. Interval between notices

        2. Class 2

Interval	Category	Overdue & 1st	1st & 2nd	2nd & 3rd	3rd & 4th	4th & 5th
1 day	Private	2 (8%)	1	0	0	0
	Public	3 (6%)	0	0	0	0
	Total	5 (7%)	1	0	0	0
2 days	Private	0	0	0	0	0
	Public	1 (2%)	0	0	0	1
	Total	1 (1%)	0	0	0	1
3 days	Private	1 (4%)	1	2	1	0
	Public	8 (16%)	3	2	1	0
	Total	9 (12%)	4	4	2	0
4 days	Private	0	0	0	0	0
	Public	3 (6%)	0	0	0	0
	Total	3 (4%)	0	0	0	0
5 days	Private	4 (16%)	0	0	0	0
	Public	4 (8%)	1	1	0	0
	Total	8 (11%)	1	1	0	0
7 days	Private	10 (40%)	10	6	1	0
	Public	15 (30%)	18	7	3	2
	Total	25 (33%)	28	13	4	2

VII. Overdue Correspondence
  B. Interval between notices
    2. Class 2 (Cont'd)

Interval	Category	Overdue & 1st	1st & 2nd	2nd & 3rd	3rd & 4th	4th & 5th
9 days	Private	0	0	0	0	0
	Public	1 (2%)	0	1	0	0
	Total	1 (1%)	0	1	0	0
2 weeks	Private	4 (16%)	8	1	0	0
	Public	7 (14%)	9	3	0	0
	Total	11 (15%)	17	4	0	0
17 days	Private	0	0	0	0	0
	Public	0	1	0	0	0
	Total	0	1	0	0	0
3 weeks	Private	0	1	0	0	0
	Public	1 (2%)	2	3	1	1
	Total	1 (1%)	3	3	1	1
1 month	Private	0	1	8	0	0
	Public	1 (2%)	4	5	1	1
	Total	1 (1%)	5	13	1	1
6 weeks	Private	0	0	0	0	0
	Public	0	1	0	0	0
	Total	0	1	0	0	0
8 weeks	Private	0	0	0	0	0
	Public	0	1	0	0	0
	Total	0	1	0	0	0
mid-se-mester	Private	1 (4%)	0	0	0	0
	Public	0	0	0	0	0
	Total	1 (1%)	0	0	0	0
end of semester	Private	0	2	2	0	0
	Public	0	3	3	0	0
	Total	0	5	5	0	0

VII. Overdue Correspondence

    B. Interval between notices

        2. Class 2 (Cont'd)

Interval	Category	Overdue & 1st	1st & 2nd	2nd & 3rd	3rd & 4th	4th & 5th
twice a year	Private	1 (2%)	1	0	0	0
	Public	0	0	0	0	0
	Total	1 (1%)	1	0	0	0
varies	Private	1 (4%)	0	0	0	0
	Public	2 (4%)	2	1	0	0
	Total	3 (4%)	2	1	0	0
not given or not applicable	Private	1 (2%)	0	6	23	25
	Public	4 (8%)	5	24	44	45
	Total	5 (7%)	5	30	67	70

VII. Overdue Correspondence

    B. Interval between notices

        3. Class 3

Interval	Category	Overdue & 1st	1st & 2nd	2nd & 3rd	3rd & 4th	4th & 5th
1 day	Private	14 (14%)	0	1	1	0
	Public	2 (6%)	1	0	0	0
	Total	16 (12%)	1	1	1	0
2 days	Private	3 (3%)	0	1	0	0
	Public	1 (3%)	0	0	0	0
	Total	4 (4%)	0	1	0	0
3 days	Private	12 (12%)	4	4	3	0
	Public	5 (15%)	2	3	2	0
	Total	17 (13%)	6	7	5	0
4 days	Private	5 (5%)	1	0	0	0
	Public	4 (12%)	0	0	0	0
	Total	9 (7%)	1	0	0	0
5 days	Private	14 (14%)	4	3	1	0
	Public	6 (18%)	1	1	1	0
	Total	20 (15%)	5	4	2	0

VII. Overdue Correspondence
  B. Interval between notices
    3. Class 3 (Cont'd)

Interval	Category	Overdue & 1st	1st & 2nd	2nd & 3rd	3rd & 4th	4th & 5th
6 days	Private	0	0	0	0	0
	Public	1 (3%)	0	0	0	0
	Total	1 (1%)	0	0	0	0
7 days	Private	23 (23%)	39	32	14	4
	Public	10 (30%)	15	8	5	1
	Total	33 (25%)	54	40	19	5
8 days	Private	0	1	0	0	0
	Public	0	0	0	0	0
	Total	0	1	0	0	0
10 days	Private	0	3	1	0	0
	Public	1 (3%)	0	0	0	0
	Total	1 (1%)	3	1	0	0
2 weeks	Private	6 (6%)	16	14	4	0
	Public	1 (3%)	5	4	2	0
	Total	7 (5%)	21	18	6	0
3 weeks	Private	4 (4%)	4	3	5	0
	Public	0	2	2	0	0
	Total	4 (3%)	6	5	5	0
1 month	Private	1 (1%)	3	6	4	1
	Public	0	3	4	0	0
	Total	1 (1%)	6	10	4	1
8 weeks	Private	1 (1%)	0	0	0	0
	Public	0	0	0	0	0
	Total	1 (1%)	0	0	0	0
mid-se-mester	Private	2 (2%)	0	0	0	0
	Public	0	0	0	0	0
	Total	2 (2%)	0	0	0	0

VII. Overdue Correspondence
   B. Interval between notices
      3. Class 3 (Cont'd)

Interval	Category	Overdue & 1st	1st & 2nd	2nd & 3rd	3rd & 4th	4th & 5th
end of semester	Private	0	2	5	15	3
	Public	0	2	1	2	2
	Total	0	4	6	17	5
twice a semester	Private	0	0	0	0	1
	Public	0	0	0	0	0
	Total	0	0	0	0	1
varies	Private	4 (4%)	5	3	2	0
	Public	0	1	2	0	0
	Total	4 (3%)	6	5	2	0
before registrat-ion	Private	0	0	0	0	0
	Public	0	0	1	0	0
	Total	0	0	1	0	0
not given or not applicable	Private	10	17	26	50	90
	Public	3	2	8	22	31
	Total	13	19	34	72	121

VII. Overdue Correspondence

   B. Interval between notices

      4. Class 4

Interval	Category	Overdue & 1st	1st & 2nd	2nd & 3rd	3rd & 4th	4th & 5th
1 day	Private	15 (14%)	3	2	0	1
	Public	4 (10%)	0	0	0	0
	Total	19 (13%)	3	2	0	1
2 days	Private	2 (2%)	0	0	0	0
	Public	0	0	0	0	0
	Total	2 (2%)	0	0	0	0
3 days	Private	21 (19%)	6	4	3	0
	Public	7 (17%)	0	1	0	0
	Total	28 (19%)	6	5	3	0
4 days	Private	5 (5%)	0	0	0	0
	Public	1 (2%)	0	0	0	0
	Total	6 (4%)	0	0	0	0
5 days	Private	9 (8%)	0	0	0	0
	Public	3 (7%)	1	1	0	0
	Total	12 (8%)	1	1	0	0
6 days	Private	1 (1%)	0	0	0	0
	Public	0	0	0	0	0
	Total	1 (1%)	0	0	0	0
7 days	Private	28 (26%)	61	43	22	4
	Public	13 (32%)	19	13	7	3
	Total	41 (27%)	80	56	29	7
8 days	Private	0	1	0	0	0
	Public	1 (2%)	0	0	0	0
	Total	1 (1%)	1	0	0	0
9 days	Private	0	0	1	0	0
	Public	0	0	0	0	0
	Total	0	0	1	0	0

VII. Overdue Correspondence
   B. Interval between notices
      4. Class 4 (Cont'd)

Interval	Category	Overdue & 1st	1st & 2nd	2nd & 3rd	3rd & 4th	4th & 5th
10 days	Private	1 (1%)	0	0	0	0
	Public	1 (2%)	0	0	0	0
	Total	2 (1%)	0	0	0	0
12 days	Private	0	0	0	1	0
	Public	0	0	0	0	0
	Total	0	0	0	1	0
2 weeks	Private	6 (6%)	9	10	6	2
	Public	3 (7%)	8	8	3	0
	Total	9 (6%)	17	18	9	2
3 weeks	Private	2 (2%)	2	3	3	0
	Public	0	0	0	0	0
	Total	2 (1%)	2	3	3	0
1 month	Private	3 (3%)	2	5	2	0
	Public	1 (2%)	2	2	0	0
	Total	4 (3%)	4	7	2	0
5 weeks	Private	0	0	0	0	0
	Public	0	1	0	0	0
	Total	0	1	0	0	0
after 1/3 semester	Private	1 (1%)	1	1	0	0
	Public	0	0	0	0	0
	Total	1 (1%)	1	1	0	0
mid-semester	Private	0	0	0	0	0
	Public	0	1	0	0	0
	Total	0	1	0	0	0
twice a semester	Private	1 (1%)	1	1	0	0
	Public	0	0	0	0	0
	Total	1 (1%)	1	1	0	0

VII. Overdue Correspondence

   B. Interval between notices

      4. Class 4 (Cont'd)

Interval	Category	Overdue & 1st	1st & 2nd	2nd & 3rd	3rd & 4th	4th & 5th
near end of semester	Private	0	0	0	0	0
	Public	0	1	0	0	0
	Total	0	1	0	0	0
end of semester	Private	0	2	6	12	8
	Public	1 (2%)	0	0	1	3
	Total	1 (1%)	2	6	13	11
varies	Private	3 (3%)	5	6	2	2
	Public	2 (5%)	3	2	1	0
	Total	5 (3%)	8	8	1	2
not given or not applicable	Private	11 (11%)	16	27	58	92
	Public	4 (9%)	5	14	29	35
	Total	15 (10%)	21	41	87	127

VII. Overdue Correspondence

   B. Interval between notices

     5. Class 5

Interval	Category	Overdue & 1st	1st & 2nd	2nd & 3rd	3rd & 4th	4th & 5th
1 day	Private	2 (8%)	0	0	0	0
	Public	0	0	0	0	0
	Total	2 (5%)	0	0	0	0
2 days	Private	0	0	0	0	0
	Public	1 (9%)	0	0	0	0
	Total	1 (3%)	0	0	0	0
3 days	Private	2 (8%)	2	1	1	0
	Public	2 (18%)	0	0	0	0
	Total	4 (11%)	2	1	1	0
4 days	Private	1 (4%)	0	0	0	0
	Public	0	0	0	0	0
	Total	1 (3%)	0	0	0	0
5 days	Private	1 (4%)	2	2	0	0
	Public	2 (18%)	0	0	0	0
	Total	3 (8%)	2	2	0	0
6 days	Private	0	0	0	0	0
	Public	1 (9%)	1	1	1	0
	Total	1 (3%)	1	1	1	0
7 days	Private	9 (35%)	12	11	2	0
	Public	4 (36%)	6	2	1	0
	Total	13 (35%)	18	13	3	0
10 days	Private	1 (4%)	1	0	0	0
	Public	0	0	0	0	0
	Total	1 (3%)	1	0	0	0
2 weeks	Private	2 (8%)	2	0	1	0
	Public	0	2	2	0	0
	Total	2 (5%)	4	2	1	0

VII. Overdue Correspondence

   B. Interval between notices

      5. Class 5 (Cont'd)

Interval	Category	Overdue & 1st	1st & 2nd	2nd & 3rd	3rd & 4th	4th & 5th
3 weeks	Private	0	0	1	1	0
	Public	0	1	1	0	0
	Total	0	1	2	1	0
1 month	Private	1 (4%)	1	0	0	0
	Public	0	0	2	1	0
	Total	1 (3%)	1	2	1	0
8 weeks	Private	0	0	0	0	0
	Public	0	0	0	1	0
	Total	0	0	0	1	0
end of semester	Private	0	0	0	3	1
	Public	0	0	0	0	0
	Total	0	0	0	3	1
varies	Private	1 (4%)	0	0	0	0
	Public	0	0	0	0	0
	Total	1 (3%)	0	0	0	0
not given or not applicable	Private	6 (23%)	6	11	18	25
	Public	1 (9%)	1	3	7	11
	Total	7 (16%)	7	14	25	36

VII. Overdue Correspondence

   B. Interval between notices

      6. All Libraries

Interval	Category	Overdue & 1st	1st & 2nd	2nd & 3rd	3rd & 4th	4th & 5th
1 day	Private	33 (12%)	4	3	1	1
	Public	9 (6%)	1	0	0	0
	Total	42 (10%)	5	3	1	1
2 days	Private	5 (2%)	0	1	0	0
	Public	3 (2%)	0	0	0	1
	Total	8 (2%)	0	1	0	1
3 days	Private	37 (14%)	14	12	8	0
	Public	24 (15%)	5	6	3	0
	Total	61 (14%)	19	18	11	0
4 days	Private	11 (4%)	1	0	0	0
	Public	12 (7%)	0	0	0	0
	Total	23 (5%)	1	0	0	0
5 days	Private	31 (11%)	6	5	1	0
	Public	16 (9%)	3	3	1	0
	Total	47 (11%)	9	8	2	0
6 days	Private	1 (-)	0	0	0	0
	Public	2 (1%)	1	1	1	0
	Total	3 (1%)	1	1	1	0
7 days	Private	74 (27%)	124	93	39	8
	Public	47 (30%)	65	33	16	6
	Total	121 (28%)	189	126	55	14
8 days	Private	1 (-)	3	1	0	0
	Public	2 (1%)	0	1	0	0
	Total	3 (1%)	3	2	0	0
9 days	Private	0	0	1	0	0
	Public	1 (-)	0	1	0	0
	Total	1 (-)	0	2	0	0

VII. Overdue Correspondence
  B. Interval between notices
    6. All Libraries (Cont'd)

Interval	Category	Overdue & 1st	1st & 2nd	2nd & 3rd	3rd & 4th	4th & 5th
10 days	Private	2 (1%)	4	1	0	0
	Public	3 (2%)	1	1	0	0
	Total	5 (1%)	5	2	0	0
12 days	Private	0	0	0	1	0
	Public	0	0	0	0	0
	Total	0	0	0	1	0
2 weeks	Private	18 (7%)	38	25	11	2
	Public	17 (11%)	25	20	7	1
	Total	35 (8%)	63	45	18	3
17 days	Private	0	0	0	0	0
	Public	0	1	0	0	0
	Total	0	1	0	0	0
3 weeks	Private	6 (2%)	7	7	9	0
	Public	1 (-)	7	6	1	1
	Total	7 (2%)	14	13	10	1
1 month	Private	7 (3%)	7	19	6	1
	Public	3 (2%)	12	14	3	1
	Total	10 (2%)	19	33	9	2
5 weeks	Private	0	0	0	0	0
	Public	0	2	1	0	0
	Total	0	2	1	0	0
6 weeks	Private	0	0	0	0	0
	Public	0	1	0	0	0
	Total	0	1	0	0	0
8 weeks	Private	1 (-)	1	0	0	0
	Public	0	1	0	1	0
	Total	1 (-)	2	0	1	0
1/3 semester	Private	1 (-)	1	1	0	0
	Public	0	0	0	0	0
	Total	1 (-)	1	1	0	0

VII. Overdue Correspondence

    B. Interval between notices

        6. All Libraries (Cont'd)

Interval	Category	Overdue & 1st	1st & 2nd	2nd & 3rd	3rd & 4th	4th & 5th
mid-semester	Private	3 (1%)	0	0	0	0
	Public	0	1	0	0	0
	Total	3 (1%)	1	0	0	0
twice a semester	Private	1 (-)	1	1	0	0
	Public	0	0	0	0	0
	Total	1 (-)	1	1	0	0
near end of semester	Private	0	0	0	0	0
	Public	0	1	0	0	0
	Total	0	1	0	0	0
end of semester	Private	0	6	14	30	12
	Public	1 (-)	6	4	3	5
	Total	1 (-)	12	18	33	17
twice a year	Private	1 (-)	1	0	0	1
	Public	0	0	0	0	0
	Total	1 (-)	1	0	0	1
before regis-tration	Private	0	0	0	0	0
	Public	0	0	1	0	0
	Total	0	0	1	0	0
varies	Private	10 (4%)	11	9	4	2
	Public	5 (3%)	6	5	1	0
	Total	15 (4%)	17	14	5	2
not given or not applicable	Private	29 (12%)	43	77	141	245
	Public	12 (8%)	18	59	119	142
	Total	41 (10%)	62	136	260	387

VII. OVERDUE CORRESPONDENCE

C. Volume of overdue correspondence - total numbers

Only slightly more than half of the reporting libraries recorded number of
notices sent. Nineteen of these, which did record overdue correspondence,
did not record circulation figures, consequently they were deleted from the
section concerned with overdue correspondence expressed as a percentage of
circulation. While libraries that do not keep statistics cannot be blamed
if they have more worthwhile things to do, the sparcity of information does
tend to diminish the value of this part.

Class	Category	Number Reporting	Number of Notices	Mean
1	Private	12	153,125	12,760
	Public	13	338,297	27,561
	Total	25	491,422	19,657
2	Private	15	103,240	4,130
	Public	31	291,289	9,396
	Total	46	394,529	8,577
3	Private	49	148,484	3,030
	Public	19	72,563	3,819
	Total	68	221,047	3,251
4	Private	51	71,678	1,405
	Public	22	16,439	747
	Total	73	88,117	1,207
5	Private	15	38,885	2,592
	Public	4	12,846	3,212
	Total	19	51,741	2,723
Total	Private	142	515,412	3,630
	Public	89	731,434	8,218
	Total	231	1,246,846	5,398

VII. Overdue Correspondence

    C. Volume of overdue correspondence - total numbers - expressed as a
       percentage of circulation

Libraries reporting circulation and overdue notices:

Class	Private	Public	Total
1	12 (93%)	13 (62%)	25 (74%)
2	15 (60%)	31 (62%)	46 (61%)
3	49 (49%)	19 (56%)	68 (51%)
4	51 (47%)	22 (54%)	73 (49%)
Total	127 (47%)	85 (54%)	212 (49%)

Class	Category	Circulation	Number of notices	Number of notices expressed as a % of circulation
1	Private	3,709,278	153,125	4.1
	Public	6,260,234	338,297	5.4
	Total	9,929,512	491,422	4.9
2	Private	2,014,312	103,240	5.1
	Public	3,862,161	291,289	7.5
	Total	5,876,473	394,529	6.7
3	Private	2,120,677	148,484	7.0
	Public	946,360	72,563	7.7
	Total	3,067,037	221,047	7.2
4	Private	549,702	71,678	13.0
	Public	240,684	16,439	6.8
	Total	790,386	88,117	11.2
Total	Private	8,393,969	476,527	5.7
	Public	11,309,439	718,588	6.4
	Total	19,703,408	1,195,115	6.1

VII. OVERDUE CORRESPONDENCE

C. Volume of overdue correspondence - expressed as a percentage of circulation

(Percentages derived from libraries reporting both circulation and number of notices (see page 50).)

Percent	Category	Class 1	Class 2	Class 3	Class 4	Total
0	Private	0	0	0	1 (2%)	1 (1%)
	Public	0	0	0	1 (5%)	1 (1%)
	Total	0	0	0	2 (3%)	2 (1%)
.1-1%	Private	1 (8%)	1 (7%)	4 (8%)	5 (10%)	11 (9%)
	Public	1 (8%)	1 (3%)	0	0	2 (2%)
	Total	2 (8%)	2 (4%)	4 (6%)	4 (6%)	13 (6%)
1-2%	Private	4 (33%)	3 (20%)	4 (8%)	4 (8%)	15 (12%)
	Public	1 (8%)	5 (17%)	2 (11%)	1 (5%)	9 (11%)
	Total	5 (20%)	8 (18%)	6 (9%)	5 (7%)	24 (12%)
2-3%	Private	0	2 (13%)	3 (6%)	4 (8%)	9 (7%)
	Public	0	4 (13%)	3 (16%)	3 (14%)	10 (12%)
	Total	0	6 (13%)	6 (9%)	7 (10%)	19 (9%)
3-4%	Private	0	1 (7%)	7 (14%)	1 (2%)	9 (7%)
	Public	4 (31%)	2 (7%)	3 (16%)	3 (16%)	12 (14%)
	Total	4 (16%)	3 (7%)	10 (15%)	4 (6%)	21 (10%)
4-5%	Private	1 (8%)	1 (7%)	4 (8%)	3 (6%)	9 (7%)
	Public	2 (15%)	4 (13%)	2 (11%)	1 (5%)	9 (11%)
	Total	3 (12%)	5 (11%)	6 (9%)	4 (6%)	18 (8%)
5-6%	Private	2 (17%)	1 (7%)	5 (10%)	1 (2%)	9 (7%)
	Public	2 (15%)	5 (17%)	0	3 (14%)	10 (12%)
	Total	4 (16%)	6 (13%)	5 (8%)	4 (6%)	19 (9%)
6-7%	Private	1 (8%)	2 (13%)	4 (8%)	2 (4%)	9 (7%)
	Public	2 (15%)	2 (7%)	1 (5%)	0	5 (6%)
	Total	3 (12%)	4 (9%)	5 (8%)	2 (3%)	14 (7%)
7-8%	Private	1 (8%)	1 (7%)	3 (6%)	3 (6%)	8 (6%)
	Public	0	0	0	2 (9%)	2 (2%)
	Total	1 (4%)	1 (2%)	3 (5%)	5 (7%)	10 (5%)

51

C. Volume of overdue correspondence - expressed as a percentage of circulation (Cont'd)

Percent	Category	Class 1	Class 2	Class 3	Class 4	Total
8-9%	Private	2 (17%)	1 (7%)	0	7 (14%)	10 (8%)
	Public	0	0	3 (16%)	1 (5%)	4 (5%)
	Total	2 (8%)	1 (2%)	3 (4%)	8 (12%)	14 (7%)
9-10%	Private	0	0	3 (6%)	1 (2%)	4 (3%)
	Public	0	0	2 (11%)	1 (5%)	3 (4%)
	Total	0	0	5 (8%)	2 (3%)	7 (3%)
10-11%	Private	0	0	2 (4%)	2 (4%)	4 (3%)
	Public	0	1 (3%)	0	1 (5%)	2 (2%)
	Total	0	1 (2%)	2 (3%)	3 (4%)	6 (3%)
11-12%	Private	0	0	1 (2%)	4 (8%)	9 (7%)
	Public	0	0	1 (5%)	2 (9%)	3 (4%)
	Total	0	0	2 (3%)	6 (8%)	12 (6%)
12-13%	Private	0	0	1 (2%)	0	1 (1%)
	Public	0	1 (3%)	0	0	1 (1%)
	Total	0	1 (2%)	1 (2%)	0	2 (1%)
14-15%	Private	0	2 (13%)	3 (6%)	2 (4%)	7 (5%)
	Public	1 (8%)	1 (3%)	1 (5%)	1 (5%)	4 (5%)
	Total	1 (4%)	3 (7%)	4 (6%)	3 (4%)	11 (5%)
14-15%	Private	0	0	1 (2%)	2 (4%)	3 (2%)
	Public	0	2 (7%)	0	0	2 (2%)
	Total	0	2 (4%)	1 (2%)	2 (3%)	5 (2%)
15-16%	Private	0	0	0	1 (2%)	1 (1%)
	Public	0	0	0	1 (5%)	1 (1%)
	Total	0	0	0	2 (3%)	2 (1%)
16-17%	Private	0	0	0	1 (2%)	1 (1%)
	Public	0	0	0	0	0
	Total	0	0	0	1 (1%)	1 (-)
17-18%	Private	0	0	0	0	0
	Public	0	1 (3%)	0	0	1 (1%)
	Total	0	1 (2%)	0	0	1 (-)

VII. Overdue Correspondence

   C. Volume of overdue correspondence - expressed as a percentage of circulation (Cont'd)

Percent	Category	Class 1	Class 2	Class 3	Class 4	Total
19-20%	Private	0	0	0	1 (2%)	1 (1%)
	Public	0	0	0	0	0
	Total	0	0	0	1 (1%)	1 (-)
20-21%	Private	0	0	0	0	0
	Public	0	1 (3%)	0	0	1 (1%)
	Total	0	1 (2%)	0	0	1 (-)
21-22%	Private	0	0	1 (2%)	1 (2%)	2 (2%)
	Public	0	0	0	0	0
	Total	0	0	1 (2%)	1 (1%)	2 (1%)
22-23%	Private	0	0	1 (2%)	1 (2%)	2 (2%)
	Public	0	0	0	1 (5%)	1 (1%)
	Total	0	0	1 (2%)	2 (3%)	3 (1%)
24-25%	Private	0	0	0	1 (2%)	1 (1%)
	Public	0	0	0	0	0
	Total	0	0	0	1 (1%)	1 (-)
30-31%	Private	0	0	0	1 (2%)	1 (1%)
	Public	0	0	0	0	0
	Total	0	0	0	1 (1%)	1 (-)
31-32%	Private	0	0	0	1 (2%)	1 (1%)
	Public	0	0	1 (5%)	0	1 (1%)
	Total	0	0	1 (2%)	1 (1%)	2 (1%)
33-34%	Private	0	0	1 (2%)	0	1 (1%)
	Public	0	0	0	0	0
	Total	0	0	1 (2%)	0	1 (-)
42-43%	Private	0	0	0	0	0
	Public	0	1 (3%)	0	0	1 (1%)
	Total	0	1 (2%)	0	0	1 (-)
45-46%	Private	0	0	0	1 (2%)	1 (1%)
	Public	0	0	0	0	0
	Total	0	0	0	1 (1%)	1 (-)

   C. Volume of overdue correspondence - expressed as a percentage of circulation (Cont'd)

Percent	Category	Class 1	Class 2	Class 3	Class 4	Total
53-54%	Private	0	0	1 (2%)	0	1 (1%)
	Public	0	0	0	0	0
	Total	0	0	1 (2%)	0	1 (-)

VIII. OVERDUE CHARGES

   The great majority of libraries surveyed charge fines, although a few
   felt that the practice was out-moded and would be abolished by them if
   only some other method of encouraging prompt return could be instituted.
   A small group of institutions even reported that in their opinion fines
   detered prompt return, although most continued to charge fines and were
   somewhat vague as to why they thought fines had the opposite of the in-
   tended effect.

   Fines and combinations thereof are presented here in condensed form, so
   as to avoid having too many single charges represented by only one library.
   In no other aspect of circulation policies does there seem to be as much
   diversity as in the charges for overdue books. Indeed, it would tax the
   imagination of any one individual to devise some of the policies reported.
   When fines for an overdue book change two, three, and even four times within a month, it is not altogether surprising that a student might not return
   a book.

   There were, within the group surveyed, some 61 different fine schedules for
   general stack books, ranging from "no fines" to a flat fine of $10.00 for
   failure to return a book within seven days. One library imposed demerits
   in lieu of fines.

   But when we get to reserve fines, the policies really become complex. It
   proved to be impossible to put into chart form the many different fines
   charged for different types of reserve books by any one library. There
   would have been more than 150 different combinations for the 417 libraries
   that reported reserve fines, consequently, for those libraries that had
   overnight books, overnight charges were recorded, and for those that did
   not have overnight books, charges for 1, 3, 7, etc. day books were recorded.

   The fines charged for reserve books ranged from "none charged" to $3.50 for
   12 hours. One library employed a "work detail" system in lieu of monetary
   fines.

VIII. OVERDUE CHARGES

A. General stack books

1. Class 1

Amount of Fine	Category	Number	Is there a relationship between fines and book return?			
			yes	no	not sure	no comment
2¢ per day	Private	1 (8%)	1			
	Public	0				
	Total	1 (3%)	1			
5¢ per day	Private	4 (31%)	2	2		
	Public	8 (38%)	7	1		
	Total	12 (35%)	9	3		
10¢ per day[1]	Private	6 (46%)	4	2		
	Public	3 (15%)	3			
	Total	9 (26%)	7	2		
15¢ per day	Private	0				
	Public	1 (5%)	1			
	Total	1 (3%)	1			
25¢ per day	Private	0				
	Public	6 (29%)	5	1		
	Total	6 (18%)	5	1		
30¢ per day	Private	1 (8%)	1			
	Public	0				
	Total	1 (3%)	1			
50¢ per 1st 3 days	Private	0				
	Public	1 (5%)			1	
	Total	1 (3%)			1	
$1.00 per day after 1st notice	Private					
	Public	1 (5%)	1			
	Total	1 (3%)	1			
$2.00 for 1st day/ 10¢ thereafter	Private					
	Public	1 (5%)		1		
	Total	1 (3%)		1		

55

VIII. Overdue Charges

   A. General stack books

      1. Class 1

Amount of Fine	Category	Number	Relationship?			
			yes	no	not sure	no comment
not given	Private	1 (8%)	1			
	Public	0				
	Total	1 (3%)	1			

	Relationship?			
Category	Yes	No	Not Sure	No Comment
Private	9 (69%)	4 (31%)		
Public	18 (85%)	2 (10%)	1 (5%)	
Total	27 (79%)	6 (18%)	1 (3%)	

1 In one private institution (yes-believes there is a relationship), fine is 5¢ per day if paid when book is returned; in another (yes), fine becomes 10¢ per day after 10 days; in a third (yes), fine increases to 25¢ per day after 7 and up to 14 days (what it is after that is not stated); and in still another private college (no) and in one public (yes), there is a $10 maximun fine imposed.

VIII. Overdue Charges

  A. General stack books

    2. Class 2

Amount of Fine	Category	Number	Relationship?			
			yes	no	not sure	no comment
none charged	Private					
	Public	3 (6%)	2	1		
	Total	3 (4%)	2	1		
2¢ per day	Private					
	Public	5 (10%)	4	1		
	Total	5 (7%)	4	1		
5¢ per day[1]	Private	11 (44%)	4	5	2	
	Public	26 (52%)	19	5	2	
	Total	37 (49%)	23	10	4	
10¢ per day[2]	Private	10 (40%)	8	1		1
	Public	5 (10%)	3	2		
	Total	15 (20%)	11	3		1
15¢ per day	Private					
	Public	1 (2%)		1		
	Total	1 (1%)		1		
25¢ per day[3]	Private	2 (8%)	1	1		
	Public	5 (10%)	5			
	Total	7 (9%)	6	1		
30¢ per day[4]	Private	1 (4%)		1		
	Public					
	Total	1 (1%)		1		
50¢ per day[5]	Private					
	Public	3 (6%)	3			
	Total	3 (4%)	3			
$1.00 per day if recalled	Private					
	Public	1 (2%)		1		
	Total	1 (1%)		1		

VIII. Overdue Charges

    A. General stack books

        2. Class 2 (Cont'd)

Amount of Fine	Category	Number	Relationship?			
			yes	no	not sure	no comment
$10 if not returned within 8 days	Private					
	Public	1 (2%)	1			
	Total	1 (1%)	1			
not given	Private	1 (4%)				1
	Public					
	Total	1 (1%)				1

	Relationship?			
Category	Yes	No	Not Sure	No Comment
Private	13 (52%)	8 (32%)	2 (8%)	2 (8%)
Public	37 (75%)	11 (22%)	2 (4%)	
Total	50 (68%)	19 (25%)	4 (5%)	2 (2%)

1 In one public college (yes), the fine is 3¢ per day if paid when book is returned.

2 In three private (all yes) and two public (one yes, one no), the fine is 5¢ per day if paid when book is returned; in one public (yes), the fine is $1.00 after the first month.

3 Fine is $1.00 per day if book has been recalled.

4 15¢ per day if paid when book is returned.

5 In one public institution (yes), the fine is 50¢ for the first day, 25¢ per day for 2 to 4 days, and 5¢ per day thereafter, with a maximun of $2.25.

VIII. Overdue Charges
  A. General stack books
    3. Class 3

Amount of Fine	Category	Number	Relationship?			
			yes	no	not sure	no comment
none charged	Private	7 (7%)	2	4	1	
	Public	2 (6%)		2		
	Total	9 (7%)	2	6	1	
2¢ per day[1]	Private	11 (11%)	7	4		
	Public	4 (12%)	2	1	1	
	Total	15 (11%)	9	5	1	
3¢ per day	Private	1 (1%)		1		
	Public					
	Total	1 (1%)		1		
4¢ per day	Private	1 (1%)	1			
	Public					
	Total	1 (1%)	1			
5¢ per day[2]	Private	61 (62%)	41	16	2	2
	Public	20 (58%)	15	2	2	1
	Total	81 (61%)	56	18	4	3
10¢ per day[3]	Private	10 (10%)	6	2	2	
	Public	5 (15%)	5			
	Total	15 (11%)	11	2	2	
15¢ per day	Private	1 (1%)	1			
	Public					
	Total	1 (1%)	1			
20¢ per day[4]	Private	1 (1%)		1		
	Public					
	Total	1 (1%)		1		
25¢ per day	Private	2 (2%)	2			
	Public	1 (3%)	1			
	Total	3 (2%)	3			
40¢ per day[5]	Private	1 (1%)	1			
	Public					
	Total	1 (1%)	1			

VIII. Overdue Charges

  A. General stack books

    3. Class 3 (Cont'd)

Amount of Fine	Category	Number	Relationship?			
			yes	no	not sure	no comment
50¢ per day[6]	Private	1 (1%)	1			
	Public					
	Total	1 (1%)	1			
$2.00 after 2nd notice	Private					
	Public	1 (3%)	1			
	Total	1 (1%)	1			
$2.00 after 3rd notice	Private	1 (1%)	1			
	Public					
	Total	1 (1%)	1			
25¢ 1st week[7]	Private	1 (1%)	1			
	Public					
	Total	1 (1%)	1			
demerits	Private					
	Public	1 (3%)	1			
	Total	1 (1%)	1			

	Relationship?			
Category	Yes	No	Not Sure	No Comment
Private	64 (65%)	28 (28%)	5 (5%)	2 (2%)
Public	25 (77%)	5 (15%)	3 (9%)	1 (3%)
Total	89 (67%)	33 (25%)	8 (6%)	3 (2%)

1 In one private college (yes), there is a maximum fine of $10.00; in another (no), the fine increases to 5¢ per day after the first five days.

2 In one private college (yes), the fine increases to 10¢ per day after the first 7 days; in one public (yes), the maximum fine charged is $1.00; in one private (yes), the fine is reduced if paid when book is returned; and in three private (all yes), the fine is halved if paid when book is returned.

3 In one public college (yes), the fine is 5¢ per day if paid when book is returned.

4 There is no charge if book is not in demand.

5 40¢ for the first 7 days, 80¢ for the next 8 days, $1.20 for the next 7 days, and for the 21st to 30th day - the price of the book + $1.00.

A. General stack books

   3. Class 3 (Cont'd)

6 The maximum fine charged is $4.00.

7 7th to 12th days, 50¢; 14th to 20th days, $1.00; 21st to 27th days, $2.00; at 28th day fine is $3.00 + postage + service charge of $3.00.

VIII. Overdue Charges

A. General stack books

   4. Class 4

Amount of Fine	Category	Number	Relationship?			
			yes	no	not sure	no comment
none charged	Private	9 (8%)	1	2	1	5
	Public	4 (10%)	3	1		
	Total	13 (9%)	4	3	1	5
1¢ per day	Private	1 (1%)	1			
	Public					
	Total	1 (1%)	1			
2¢ per day[1]	Private	13 (12%)	10	3		
	Public	4 (10%)	2	1	1	
	Total	17 (11%)	12	4	1	
3¢ per day	Private	4 (4%)	2	1	1	
	Public					
	Total	4 (3%)	2	1	1	
5¢ per day[2]	Private	60 (55%)	35	20	5	
	Public	22 (53%)	14	8		
	Total	82 (55%)	49	28	5	
10¢ per day[3]	Private	14 (13%)	10	3	1	
	Public	3 (7%)	1	2		
	Total	17 (11%)	11	5	1	
15¢ per day	Private					
	Public	1 (2%)		1		
	Total	1 (1%)		1		

VIII. Overdue Charges

    A. General stack books

        5. Class 5 (Cont'd)

Amount of Fine	Category	Number	Relationship?			
			yes	no	not sure	no comment
25¢ per day	Private					
	Public	1 (9%)			1	
	Total	1 (3%)			1	
$1.00 after 1st notice	Private	1 (4%)	1			
	Public					
	Total	1 (3%)	1			
footnote 2	Private	1 (4%)	1			
	Public					
	Total	1 (3%)	1			

	Relationship?			
Category	Yes	No	Not Sure	No Comment
Private	15 (58%)	8 (31%)	3 (11%)	
Public	4 (36%)	4 (36%)	3 (28%)	
Total	19 (51%)	12 (32%)	6 (17%)	

1 In one private college (yes), the maximum fine charged is $1.50; in another (yes), the maximum fine charged is $2.50.

2 There is no charge for the first notice, $1.00 for the second notice (regardless of the number of books involved), $3.00 for the third notice + a $5.00 processing fee + current cost of the book(s), if book(s) are not returned within two days of the third notice.

VIII. Overdue Charges
  A. General stack books
    6. All Libraries

Amount of Fine	Category	Number	Relationship?			
			yes	no	not sure	no comment
none charged	Private	19 (7%)	3	9	2	5
	Public	9 (6%)	5	4		
	Total	28 (7%)	8	13	2	5
1¢ per day	Private	1 (-)	1			
	Public					
	Total	1 (-)	1			
2¢ per day	Private	29 (11%)	19	8	2	
	Public	14 (9%)	8	4	2	
	Total	43 (10%)	27	12	4	
3¢ per day	Private	6 (2%)	3	2	1	
	Public					
	Total	6 (1%)	3	2	1	
4¢ per day	Private	1 (-)	1			
	Public					
	Total	1 (-)	1			
5¢ per day	Private	145 (53%)	88	46	9	2
	Public	82 (52%)	57	19	5	1
	Total	227 (53%)	145	65	14	3
10¢ per day	Private	47 (17%)	34	8	4	1
	Public	18 (11%)	13	4	1	
	Total	65 (15%)	47	12	5	1
15¢ per day	Private	1 (-)	1			
	Public	4 (3%)	2	2		
	Total	5 (1%)	3	2		
20¢ per day	Private	1 (-)		1		
	Public					
	Total	1 (-)		1		

VIII. Overdue Charges

    A. General stack books

        6. All Libraries (Cont'd)

Amount of Fine	Category	Number	Relationship?			
			Yes	No	Not Sure	No Comment
none charged up to but less than 10¢ per day	Private	201 (74%)[1]	115 (57%)	65 (32%)	14 (7%)	7 (4%)
	Public	105 (67%)	70 (67%)	27 (25%)	7 (7%)	1 (1%)
	Total	306 (71%)	185 (60%)[2]	93 (30%)	21 (7%)	8 (3%)
10¢ per day up to but less than 25¢ per day	Private	49 (18%)	35 (71%)	9 (18%)	4 (4%)	1 (3%)
	Public	22 (14%)	15 (68%)	6 (27%)	1 (5%)	0
	Total	71 (17%)	50 (71%)	15 (21%)	5 (7%)	1 (1%)
25¢ per day up to but less than 50¢ per day	Private	10 (4%)	7 (70%)	3 (30%)	0	0
	Public	16 (10%)	12 (75%)	3 (19%)	1 (6%)	0
	Total	26 (6%)	19 (73%)	6 (23%)	1 (4%)	0
50¢ per day and over	Private	5 (2%)	4 (80%)	1 (20%)	0	0
	Public	12 (8%)	9 (75%)	2 (17%)	1 (8%)	0
	Total	17 (4%)	13 (76%)	3 (18%)	1 (6%)	0
others and not given	Private	7 (3%)	3 (43%)	1 (14%)	1 (14%)	2 (29%)
	Public	2 (1%)	1 (50%)	1 (50%)	0	0
	Total	9 (2%)	4 (44%)	2 (22%)	1 (11%)	2 (22%)
all	Private	272 (100%)	164 (60%)	79 (29%)	19 (7%)	10 (4%)
	Public	157 (100%)	107 (68%)	39 (25%)	10 (6%)	1 (1%)
	Total	429 (100%)	271 (63%)	118 (28%)	29 (7%)	11 (2%)

1 201 of the 272 private institutions in the survey.

2 Percentages are based on the number of institutions within each field, e.g., 185 or 60% of the 306 that charged less than 10¢ per day thought there was a relationship.

68

VIII. Overdue Charges

  B. Fines for reserve books

    1. Class 1

Amount Charged 1st phase	Category	Number/ Percentage	Phase 2 Fine increases or decreases, etc.
none charged	Private	1 (8%)	
	Public		
	Total	1 (3%)	
10¢ per hour	Private		
	Public	1 (5%)	
	Total	1 (3%)	
25¢ per hour	Private	2 (15%)	
	Public	5 (24%)[1]	
	Total	7 (21%)	
25¢ per 1st hour	Private	1 (8%)	
	Public	1 (5%)	increases after 1st hour
	Total	2 (6%)	
25¢ per 1st hour	Private	1 (8%)	
	Public	4 (19%)	decreases after 1st hour
	Total	5 (16%)	
25¢ per 1st 4 hours	Private		
	Public	1 (5%)	decreases thereafter
	Total	1 (3%)	
30¢ per hour	Private		
	Public	1 (5%)	
	Total	1 (3%)	
40¢ per hour	Private		
	Public	1 (5%)	
	Total	1 (3%)	
50¢ per hour	Private	1 (8%)	
	Public		
	Total	1 (3%)	

VIII. Overdue Charges
  B. Fines for reserve books
     2. Class 2 (Cont'd)

Amount Charged 1st phase	Category	Number/ Percentage	Phase 2 Fine increases and decreases, etc.
50¢ 1st hour	Private		
	Public	1 (2%)	maximum fine imposed
	Total	1 (1%)	
50¢ 1st hour	Private	2 (8%)[2]	
	Public	3 (6%)	decreases after 1st hour
	Total	5 (7%)	
50¢ per hour, 1st and 2nd hours	Private		
	Public	1 (2%)	decreases thereafter
	Total	1 (1%)	
50¢ per 1st ½ hour	Private		
	Public	1 (2%)	decreases thereafter; $1.50 maximum fine
	Total	1 (1%)	
$1.00 per hour	Private		
	Public	1 (2%)	
	Total	1 (1%)	
$1.00 per 1st hour	Private		
	Public	1 (2%)	15¢ per hour 1st day; $1.00 per day for 4 days; $1.00 per month thereafter
	Total	1 (1%)	
35¢ per day	Private		
	Public	1 (2%)	25¢ per day if paid when book is returned
	Total	1 (1%)	
50¢ per day	Private	1 (4%)	
	Public	1 (2%)	
	Total	2 (3%)	
50¢ 1st day	Private		
	Public	1 (2%)	decreases after 1st day
	Total	1 (1%)	
$1.00 per day	Private		
	Public	1 (2%)	
	Total	1 (1%)	

72

VIII. Overdue Charges
  B. Fines for reserve books
    2. Class 2 (Cont'd)

Amount Charged 1st phase	Category	Number/ Percentage	Phase 2 Fine increases or decreases, etc.
$2.25 per day	Private	1 (4%)	
	Public		
	Total	1 (1%)	
$2.50 per day	Private	1 (4%)	
	Public		
	Total	1 (1%)	
$3.50 per day	Private		
	Public	1 (2%)	
	Total	1 (1%)	
not given	Private	6 (24%)	
	Public	1 (2%)	
	Total	7 (9%)	
not specific	Private	4 (16%)	
	Public	8 (16%)	
	Total	12 (16%)	

1 In this group, four public institutions imposed a maximum fine, ranging from
   50¢ to $5.00

2 In this group, one private institution imposed a maximum fine of $2.50.

VIII. Overdue Charges
   B. Fines for reserve books
      3. Class 3 (Cont'd)

Amount Charged 1st phase	Category	Number/ Percentage	Phase 2 Fine increases or decreases, etc.
25¢ per day	Private	2 (2%)	
	Public	1 (3%)	
	Total	3 (2%)	
50¢ per day	Private	1 (1%)	
	Public		
	Total	1 (1%)	
50¢ 1st day	Private	1 (1%)	
	Public		decreases after 1st day
	Total	1 (1%)	
$3.00 for up to 12 hours	Private		
	Public	1 (3%)	$5.00 for over 12 hours
	Total	1 (1%)	
demerits	Private		
	Public	1 (3%)	
	Total	1 (1%)	
not given	Private	1 (1%)	
	Public	1 (3%)	
	Total	2 (2%)	
not specific	Private	23 (23%)	
	Public	3 (9%)	
	Total	26 (20%)	

1 In this group, one public institution does not charge any fine for the first 12 hours.

2 In this group, one public institution charges 10¢ per hour if the fine is paid when the book is returned.

3 In this group, one private institution imposes a maximum fine.

4 In this group, three private institutions impose a maximum fine.

5 In this group, one private institution imposes a maximum fine.

VIII. Overdue Charges

   B. Fines for reserve books

      4. Class 4

Amount Charged 1st phase	Category	Number/ Percentage	Phase 2 Fine increases or decreases, etc.
none charged	Private	11 (10%)	
	Public	5 (12%)	
	Total	16 (11%)	
5¢ per hour	Private	4 (4%)	
	Public	1 (2%)	
	Total	5 (3%)	
10¢ per hour[1]	Private	8 (7%)	
	Public		
	Total	8 (5%)	
10¢ 1st hour	Private	1 (1%)	
	Public		decreases after 1st hour
	Total	1 (1%)	
10¢ 1st hour	Private	1 (1%)	
	Public		increases after 1st hour
	Total	1 (1%)	
10¢ per hour, 1st and 2nd hours	Private	1 (1%)	
	Public		decreases thereafter
	Total	1 (1%)	
15¢ per hour	Private		
	Public	1 (2%)	
	Total	1 (1%)	
20¢ per hour	Private	1 (1%)	
	Public		
	Total	1 (1%)	
25¢ per hour[2]	Private	14 (13%)	
	Public	13 (32%)	
	Total	27 (18%)	
25¢ 1st hour[3]	Private	19 (17%)	
	Public	6 (15%)	decreases after 1st hour
	Total	25 (17%)	

VIII. Overdue Charges
B. Fines for reserve books
5. Class 5

Amount Charged 1st phase	Category	Number/ Percentage	Phase 2 Fine increases or decreases, etc.
none charged	Private	3 (12%)	
	Public		
	Total	3 (8%)	
10¢ per hour	Private	2 (8%)	
	Public	1 (9%)	
	Total	3 (8%)	
20¢ per hour	Private	1 (5%)	
	Public		
	Total	1 (3%)	
25¢ per hour	Private	5 (19%)	
	Public	4 (36%)	
	Total	9 (24%)	
25¢ 1st hour	Private	2 (8%)	
	Public	2 (18%)	decreases after 1st hour
	Total	4 (11%)	
10¢ 1st day or hour	Private	1 (4%)	
	Public		decreases after 1st day
	Total	1 (3%)	
25¢ per ½ day	Private	1 (4%)	
	Public		
	Total	1 (3%)	
25¢ per day after 1st day	Private	1 (4%)	
	Public		
	Total	1 (3%)	
$1.00 per day	Private	1 (4%)	
	Public		
	Total	1 (3%)	
$2.00 per day	Private	1 (4%)	
	Public		
	Total	1 (3%)	

80

VIII. Overdue Charges

    B. Fines for reserve books

       5. Class 5 (Cont'd)

Amount Charged 1st phase	Category	Number/ Percentage	Phase 2 Fine increases or decreases, etc.
not specific	Private	8 (31%)	
	Public	4 (36%)	
	Total	12 (32%)	

VIII. Overdue Charges

    B. Fines for reserve books

       6. All Classes

Amount Charged 1st phase	Category	Number/ Percentage	Phase 2 Fine increases or decreases, etc.
none charged	Private	19 (7%)	
	Public	8 (5%)	
	Total	27 (6%)	
5¢ per hour[1]	Private	6 (2%)	
	Public	7 (4%)	
	Total	13 (3%)	
10¢ per hour	Private	15 (6%)	
	Public	8 (5%)	
	Total	23 (5%)	
10¢ 1st hour	Private	1 (-)	
	Public		increases after 1st hour
	Total	1 (-)	
10¢ 1st hour	Private	1 (-)	
	Public		decreases after 1st hour
	Total	1 (-)	
10¢ per hour, 1st & 2nd hours	Private	1 (-)	
	Public		decreases thereafter
	Total	1 (-)	
15¢ per hour	Private	1 (-)	
	Public	1 (-)	
	Total	2 (-)	

VIII. Overdue Charges

   B. Fines for reserve books

      6. All Classes (Cont'd)

Amount Charged 1st phase	Category	Number/ Percentage	Phase 2 Fine increases or decreases, etc.
50¢ 1st ½ hour	Private		decreases thereafter; maximum fine imposed
	Public	1 (-)	
	Total	1 (-)	
$1.00 per hour	Private	1 (-)	
	Public	2 (1%)	
	Total	3 (1%)	
$1.00 1st hour	Private		decreases after 1st hour
	Public	1 (-)	
	Total	1 (-)	
$1.00 1st hour	Private		15¢ per hour 1st day; $1.00 per day for 4 days; $1.00 per month thereafter
	Public	1 (-)	
	Total	1 (-)	
$2.00 1st hour	Private		decreases after 1st hour
	Public	1 (-)	
	Total	1 (-)	
2¢ per day	Private	1 (-)	
	Public		
	Total	1 (-)	
5¢ per day	Private	1 (-)	
	Public		
	Total	1 (-)	
10¢ per day	Private	1 (-)	
	Public		
	Total	1 (-)	
10¢ 1st day or hour	Private	1 (-)	decreases thereafter
	Public		
	Total	1 (-)	
20¢ 1st day	Private		
	Public	1 (-)	
	Total	1 (-)	

84

VIII. Overdue Charges

  B. Fines for reserve books

    6. All Classes (Cont'd)

Amount Charged 1st phase	Category	Number/ Percentage	Phase 2 Fine increases or decreases, etc.
25¢ per day	Private	2 (1%)	
	Public	1 (-)	
	Total	3 (1%)	
25¢ per day, after 1st day	Private	1 (-)	
	Public		
	Total	1 (-)	
35¢ per day	Private		
	Public	1 (-)	25¢ per day if paid when book is returned
	Total	1 (-)	
25¢ per ½ day	Private	1 (-)	
	Public		
	Total	1 (-)	
50¢ per day	Private	3 (1%)	
	Public	1 (-)	
	Total	4 (1%)	
50¢ 1st day	Private	1 (-)	
	Public	1 (-)	
	Total	2 (-)	
75¢ per day	Private		
	Public	1 (-)	
	Total	1 (-)	
$1.00 per day	Private	2 (1%)	
	Public	2 (1%)	
	Total	4 (1%)	
$1.65 per day	Private	1 (-)	
	Public		
	Total	1 (-)	
$2.00 per day	Private	2 (1%)	
	Public		
	Total	2 (-)	

There is a Relationship (with or without comment)	Category	Class 1	Class 2	Class 3	Class 4	Class 5	Total
no comment offered	Private	3 (23%)	4 (16%)	27 (27%)	25 (23%)	5 (19%)	64 (25%)
	Public	8 (38%)	7 (14%)	8 (24%)	7 (17%)	2 (18%)	32 (20%)
	Total	11 (32%)	11 (15%)	35 (26%)	32 (21%)	7 (19%)	96 (22%)
fines discourage borrowers from returning books	Private	0	0	0	0	0	0
	Public	0	1 (2%)	0	2 (5%)	0	3 (2%)
	Total	0	1 (1%)	0	2 (1%)	0	3 (1%)
even high fines are not effective	Private	0	1 (4%)	2 (2%)	0	1 (4%)	4 (1%)
	Public	0	0	0	0	0	0
	Total	0	1 (1%)	2 (1%)	0	1 (3%)	4 (1%)
even increasing fines are not effective	Private	0	0	1 (1%)	0	0	1 (-)
	Public	0	0	0	0	0	0
	Total	0	0	1 (1%)	0	0	1 (-)
fines (generally) are not an effective means of encouraging return	Private	0	6 (24%)	13 (13%)	19 (17%)	7 (27%)	45 (17%)
	Public	2 (9%)	2 (4%)	4 (12%)	8 (20%)	4 (36%)	20 (13%)
	Total	2 (6%)	8 (11%)	17 (13%)	27 (18%)	11 (30%)	65 (15%)
fines very definitely are an effective means of encouraging return	Private	0	1 (4%)	0	0	1 (4%)	2 (1%)
	Public	0	0	1 (3%)	0	0	1 (-)
	Total	0	1 (1%)	1 (1%)	0	1 (3%)	3 (1%)
high fines (25¢ per day or more) are effective	Private	1 (8%)	0	8 (8%)	6 (5%)	3 (11%)	18 (7%)
	Public	2 (10%)	9 (18%)	3 (9%)	2 (5%)	0	16 (10%)
	Total	3 (9%)	9 (12%)	11 (8%)	8 (5%)	3 (8%)	34 (8%)
very high fines may be effective	Private	1 (8%)	0	0	0	0	1 (-)
	Public	0	0	1 (3%)	0	0	1 (-)
	Total	1 (3%)	0	1 (1%)	0	0	2 (-)
raising fines increase their effectiveness	Private	2 (15%)	1 (4%)	4 (4%)	4 (4%)	1 (4%)	12 (4%)
	Public	4 (20%)	2 (4%)	1 (3%)	2 (5%)	0	9 (6%)
	Total	6 (18%)	3 (4%)	5 (4%)	6 (4%)	1 (3%)	21 (5%)
fines (generally) are an effective means of encouraging return	Private	0	1 (4%)	22 (22%)	23 (21%)	2 (8%)	48 (18%)
	Public	0	2 (4%)	4 (12%)	5 (12%)	2 (18%)	13 (8%)
	Total	0	3 (4%)	26 (20%)	28 (19%)	4 (11%)	61 (14%)

There is a Relationship (with or without comment)	Category	Class 1	Class 2	Class 3	Class 4	Class 5	Total
even small fines are effective	Private	0	0	0	0	0	0
	Public	0	1 (2%)	0	0	0	1 (-)
	Total	0	1 (1%)	0	0	0	1 (-)
fines are somewhat effective	Private	0	1 (4%)	0	0	0	1 (-)
	Public	0	1 (2%)	1 (3%)	0	0	2 (1%)
	Total	0	2 (3%)	1 (1%)	0	0	3 (1%)
fines are slightly effective	Private	0	0	0	1 (1%)	0	1 (-)
	Public	0	0	0	4 (10%)	0	4 (3%)
	Total	0	0	0	5 (3%)	0	5 (1%)
fines should be abolished but are somewhat effective	Private	1 (8%)	0	0	0	0	1 (-)
	Public	0	0	0	0	0	0
	Total	1 (3%)	0	0	0	0	1 (-)
not effective because too low (would be effective if higher)	Private	1 (8%)	0	2 (2%)	0	0	3 (1%)
	Public	0	1 (2%)	1 (3%)	0	0	2 (1%)
	Total	1 (3%)	1 (1%)	3 (2%)	0	0	5 (1%)
fines may be an effective means of encouraging return	Private	0	1 (4%)	0	0	0	1 (-)
	Public	0	5 (10%)	1 (3%)	0	0	6 (4%)
	Total	0	6 (8%)	1 (1%)	0	0	7 (2%)
reducing fines discourages return	Private	0	0	0	0	0	0
	Public	1 (5%)	0	0	0	0	1 (1%)
	Total	1 (3%)	0	0	0	0	1 (-)
threat of a fine is[1] an effective means of encouraging return	Private	0	0	0	1 (1%)	0	1 (-)
	Public	1 (5%)	1 (2%)	0	0	0	2 (1%)
	Total	1 (3%)	1 (1%)	0	1 (1%)	0	3 (1%)
withholding borrowing privileges more effective than fines	Private	0	0	0	0	0	0
	Public	0	1 (2%)	0	0	0	1 (-)
	Total	0	1 (1%)	0	0	0	1 (-)
external influence[2] more effective than fines	Private	1 (8%)	3 (12%)	7 (7%)	4 (4%)	1 (4%)	16 (6%)
	Public	0	4 (8%)	2 (6%)	3 (7%)	0	9 (6%)
	Total	1 (3%)	7 (9%)	9 (7%)	7 (5%)	1 (3%)	25 (6%)